Ready for Learning and Ready for Life

Ready for Learning and Ready for Life

Bridging the Disconnects Between Research and Practice

Betsy Gunzelmann

ROWMAN & LITTLEFIELD
Lanham • Boulder • New York • London

Published by Rowman & Littlefield
A wholly owned subsidiary of The Rowman & Littlefield Publishing Group, Inc.
4501 Forbes Boulevard, Suite 200, Lanham, Maryland 20706
www.rowman.com

Unit A, Whitacre Mews, 26-34 Stannary Street, London SE11 4AB

Copyright © 2017 by Betsy Gunzelmann

All rights reserved. No part of this book may be reproduced in any form or by any electronic or mechanical means, including information storage and retrieval systems, without written permission from the publisher, except by a reviewer who may quote passages in a review.

British Library Cataloguing in Publication Information Available

Library of Congress Cataloging-in-Publication Data Available

ISBN 978-1-4758-1540-5 (cloth : alk. paper)
ISBN 978-1-4758-1541-2 (pbk. : alk. paper)
ISBN 978-1-4758-1542-9 (electronic)

∞™ The paper used in this publication meets the minimum requirements of American National Standard for Information Sciences—Permanence of Paper for Printed Library Materials, ANSI/NISO Z39.48-1992.

Printed in the United States of America

This book is dedicated to all those young students who have struggled due to a lack of preparation that was required for their needs, and to their worried parents and dedicated teachers.

Contents

Preface	ix
Acknowledgments	xi

PART I: UNDERSTANDING THE CONCEPT OF BEING READY AND THE DISCONNECTS — 1

1	What Is Being Ready All About?	3
2	The Paradoxes and Disconnects	9
3	Catalysts to Our Understanding: Theoretical and Research Foundations	15
4	A Current Understanding of Development for Readiness	23

PART II: THE SYNERGISTIC READINESS — 29

5	The Physical Piece	31
6	The Cognitive Piece	37
7	The Emotional Piece	41
8	The Core Piece	47
9	The Behavioral Piece	53
10	The Environmental Piece	57
11	The Synergistic Process	63

PART III: THE INTERVENTIONS AND DISCUSSIONS: RESEARCH-BASED INTERVENTIONS TO PROMOTE READINESS FOR LEARNING AND FOR LIFE— THE PARADOXES CAN BE RESOLVED AND GAPS CAN BE BRIDGED!   **69**

12 Getting Ready Physically: Predominantly Physically Based Interventions   71

13 Getting Ready Cognitively: Mainly Cognitive Interventions   79

14 Getting Ready Emotionally: Largely Emotional-Based Interventions   83

15 Getting Ready with Our Center: Chiefly Core Interventions   91

16 Getting Ready Behaviorally: Generally Behavioral Interventions   97

17 Getting Ready Environmentally: Essentially Environmental Interventions   101

PART IV: BRINGING IT ALL TOGETHER AND HOPE FOR THE FUTURE   **107**

18 Ready for Learning and Ready for Life in a Nutshell   109

19 So Where Do We Go From Here???   113

References and Suggested Reading   115

Notes   123

About the Author   125

Preface

This book is intended to be a "call to arms" reaching out to those in positions of educational leadership and reform as well as those on the front lines, including superintendents, teachers, and parents. The writing of this book is based upon solid theory and current research, along with knowledge and skills developed from several workshops sponsored by the Harvard Medical School and others approved by the American Psychological Association (APA).

Additionally, as a licensed psychologist and college/university professor with almost thirty years of experience in teaching, researching, and writing, and having observed individuals for many years over several stages of life, including young students, college and graduate-level learners, and early career professionals, has solidified my understanding of these populations. The process of researching and writing this book involved a personal journey, bringing me back to my early childhood, family, friends, and schooling. The memories of failures and successes, the psychological injuries and triumphs, were reexamined from a mature perspective.

This synthesized outcome provides the necessary lens through which we can see what is really hindering many children in schools today, along with possible approaches and interventions, typically not seen as educational in nature, but may be just the needed prescription to our ailing youth.

Although the main focus of this book is to help prepare school-aged students and those preparing to enter higher education, my intent is to try to help all folks, regardless of age, learn and thrive. *Ready for Learning and Ready for Life* offers optimism and opportunity for positive changes. Through reflection, reevaluation, and application of research-based approaches, my hope is that it encourage all of us to make changes for the better, and ultimately improve our future.

Acknowledgments

I have been so fortunate over the last many years, having the ongoing belief in my research and writing from Tom Koerner at Rowman & Littlefield Education, along with his team members, especially Carlie Wall, Bethany Janka, Anita Singh and her team members and all of the people involved who actually make this work available to those who may benefit most from this manuscript: students, parents, teachers, and the general public. Their professionalism, patience, and caring approach make it a pleasure to work with them.

Furthermore, the continued support from my administrators, colleagues, and work with students at Southern NH University has allowed me to continue to do what I love: research and writing. Without their assistance for professional development, this work would not have been possible.

It also goes without saying that my son, Matt, continues to be a source of inspiration as he exhibits the readiness needed to be ready for learning and for life.

Part I

UNDERSTANDING THE CONCEPT OF BEING READY AND THE DISCONNECTS

"The readiness to initiate the journey cannot be forced nor can people be faulted if it has not occurred in them as yet. The level of consciousness has to have advanced to the stage where such an intention would be meaningful and attractive."

David Hawkins

Chapter 1

What Is Being Ready All About?

When the students don't learn, the school must change.

—Bill Gates

READY, SET, GO! NO!

Some may ask, "Aren't we ready already?" "Not by a long shot!" And we cannot place the total responsibility on our schools and teachers alone, but it is our collective responsibility as parents, educators, medical professionals, researchers, policy makers, and community members to help each other thrive.

Getting ready for learning and ready for life does not imply a time schedule, start and finish lines, or a race to be first. Rather it means developing a way of being, that is, a process that can be taught and nurtured within each child to indeed be ready for learning and ready for life. This process addresses the psychological aspects of readiness, learning, and adaptation, allowing children to be ready for learning and ready for challenges and transitions in life.

In education and psychology, the term "readiness" has often been used as "a developmental stage at which a child has the capacity to receive instruction at a given level of difficulty or to engage in a particular activity." (http://www.dictionary.com/browse/readiness)

When speaking of readiness in this book, the definition goes beyond what our schools typically assess to determine readiness to attend school, which is often based on age. There is so much more to readiness than this and so much more we can do to help everyone be better prepared to learn and cope throughout the lifetime.

From my previous research and writing, it became evident that there is a serious aspect of our children that was neglected in our culture and in our academic preparation. It is the psychological development of our children that is overlooked; their emotional, cognitive, behavioral, and spiritual aspects take a back seat to the accumulation of facts and knowledge without the proper preparation for learning or the needed ability to cope with life's challenges and transitions.

There are numerous possible reasons for this disregard, many of which have been identified from research and writing my previous books. For example, it is clear that our schools have to work much of the time in a crisis mode, playing catch-up to our global neighbors who are soaring academically or to prevent and intervene if disasters strike. Although most of our schools have solid curriculum, objectives, materials, technology and dedicated teachers—although there definitely are inequities and many of our students still do not seem to be thriving.

It appears we have many paradoxes and disconnects such as the rift between research data and what is practiced in our schools. Thus, it is time to write about these issues and suggest positive approaches that help bridge these gaps while enhancing the atmosphere for students and teachers alike. Furthermore, it can even help our young adults get ready for the transition to college, the world of work, and all of life's transitions and challenges.

This process is called "a better way of being," which ideally should be introduced to children at a very young age. A better way of being sets the stage and establishes a solid foundation for learning and for coping now and throughout life. What is most intriguing about this process is it is not dogmatic in any way. Depending upon one's culture, individual beliefs, gender, and strengths or limitations, the research and age-old practices offer numerous ways to help all children be ready for learning and ready for life. There is no one-size-fits-all approach, but there most definitely is a need to help our children with their psychological and physical mind/body development in order to thrive academically and be successful in life.

Addressing these psychological needs and preparing for readiness involve teaching a realistic, yet optimistic mindset and behavior. We are not talking about putting on rose-colored glasses, but about teaching optimism and resilience to children in a manner similar to the approach well researched and documented by Martin E.P. Seligman. In order to do this, we need to realize that we have a choice in how we think and react.

For example, if a child interprets his difficulty in learning math facts to believing he/she is stupid, then this may generalize to other subjects sabotaging learning overall. Instead, if he understands that he may learn differently than others, but indeed can learn, we may have a very different outcome. Each of us has the ability to choose to respond otherwise to situations, and this can be taught and learned, increasing a child's resilience as suggested by Seligman (1990; 1998; 2006; 2011).

We are also talking about using a more mindful approach. Psychiatrist Daniel J. Siegel (2007) states:

> We are in desperate need of a new way of being—in ourselves, in our schools, and in our society. Our modern cultures has evolved at times to create a troubled world with individuals suffering from alienation, schools failing to inspire and to connect with students, in short, a society without a moral compass to help clarify how we can move forward in our global community. (p. xv)

Mindfulness is an age-old practice with new cutting-edge research evidence demonstrating the physical, psychological, and social benefits. Learning mindful approaches—learning to be more attuned to all that is happening within and around ourselves—allows us to be fully involved in the experience of learning to understand self and others better. This can foster empathy and acceptance helping our schools become "bully proof" and safer.

In addition, there are physical ways to cultivate a better way of being. For example, yoga is one such approach that helps connect mind-body interactions, while improving physical health, well-being, and attention to the present moment (a very necessary condition for learning).

Other forms of exercise have also proven results with children in schools, but have yet to be applied in a comprehensive manner. Dr. John Ratey's (2008) research indicates there is a positive connection between exercise and brain performance; exercise improves one's ability to learn, counters high stress levels, and helps reduce and even prevent maladaptive anxiety, reduces depression, while increasing levels of focus and attention.

Furthermore, specific fields of study such as art and music aid children to be ready for learning. Emphasis should be laid on these areas because currently there is a movement away from the arts and humanities, and they are seen as less important than the science, technology, engineering, and mathematics (STEM) subjects. In fact, it is the arts that can help our children excel in the STEM areas; without the arts and humanities, our children will be less well prepared.

Although we will get into the specifics in more detail in upcoming chapters, it is essential to highlight just how important these areas are with being ready. Gaab, Tallal, Kim, Lakshminarayanan, Archie, Glover & Gabrieli (2005) have illustrated that musical training has been demonstrated to increase verbal memory and reading ability in children and adults. Furthermore, Immordino-Yang & Damasio (2007) discuss "emotional thought" which is highly related to learning, attention and memory, decision-making, and social functioning. These are also strongly affected by emotion and should have direct impact on how we teach.

We also know that at certain times in human development, some subjects are easier to learn (i.e., foreign languages earlier). Our brains are much more plastic than realized previously, yet we also need to take into account that learning may be more difficult and resistant at certain times in one's development. Stamm (2007) specifies the need to teach children at the time developmentally and provide information correctly the first time!

We need to help children learn how to self-understand, self-regulate, and focus. (This does not mean that all children with serious attention problems may not benefit from medication due to a true neurological condition, but many can be supported with other approaches as well.)

Children also need to become socially involved to develop the psychosocial aspects of self. When children become socially involved in a caring and responsible manner, the brain is stimulated in a healthy manner and deep learning and reinforcement occur. Neurologist R. Tanzi and Dr. D. Chopra assert: "The issue is the rewards you receive through bonding and connection, the basic process that makes a peaceful social engagement is important as is intellectual/stimulation for health of brain ... and helps to make a more peaceful society" (p. 301).

The social connections are extremely important to the overall psychological health of the child too. Psychiatrist E. Hallowell expresses that the benefit students can obtain from becoming involved with others is significant. He believes that connection is a very important factor to prevent problems from developing. If a child feels connected at both home and school, he/she is not likely to get into trouble.

Alternate approaches need to be considered with the understanding that most teachers already possess that a one-size-fits-all approach to teaching will not work with all children. And indeed some very nontraditional approaches have been demonstrated to show remarkable results when approaches such as animal-assisted learning and therapy. Some children (and adults for that matter) may connect better with animals and have shown to make remarkable progress in language, learning, and even with physical and psychological gains through assistance from animals. We shall see just how important flexibility is when helping others become ready for learning and ready for life.

Although the research result may be mixed with the use of animals, it is clear that some animals' senses are more penetrating than those of humans, and the benefits can be more far reaching than once thought. Have benefit for many individuals without harmful side effects. We are never going to be 100% sure of any approach partly due to each person's uniqueness and partly due to error variance with all research practices.

But let me be very clear and cautionary here: we should not use any approach just because it appears to work or trust any charlatan that proposes he can cure all learning and living problems. The concepts you will find within this book often date back thousands of years, and might indeed embrace the wisdom and knowledge accumulated from various cultures. So you see the gap is not just between teachers and researchers, it is between our way of thinking. Yes, all these need to be backed up with ongoing research, but our researchers should focus on the right areas, and all of us need to have an open mind and the willingness to consider different ways of learning to promote growth and an overall better way of being.

Young people are at serious risk academically and psychologically. The tremendous stress that youth are put under due to developmental changes, along with the pressure from teachers, parents, peers, and competition in the global arena can be overwhelming emotionally and destructive to the learning process. It is up to us to provide them with a better way of being—based upon solid research—that will allow them to grow, learn, and flourish.

Thus, are we ready to embark on readings that may lead to a better understanding of what our children need in order to be ready for learning, ready for life?

Chapter 2

The Paradoxes and Disconnects

We are faced with the paradoxical fact that education has become one of the chief obstacles to intelligence and freedom of thought.

—Bertrand A. Russell (1872–1970)

Carl Jung was a brilliant intellect, possibly more aware of the many paradoxes of life than any other. One area he struggled with was the problem that science, with its need for rationality and preciseness, often overlooked the other aspects of life. These facets are not explainable in terms of logic, but are nonetheless a part of our world and our lives and thus should not be delegated to a lower standard or ignored. Our psyche, emotions, cognitions, and at times our behaviors are all very much subject to the irrationality and inexactitude of humans.

It seems that attempting to understand how best to help children become ready for learning and ready for life, a very human process, is no less full of life's many paradoxes. Here the focus is on a few that seem central, yet perplexing, to our purpose of being ready for learning and ready for life.

On the one hand we live in a busy, advanced, productive, and accountable society. On the other hand, the consequences of our fast-paced culture result in a highly stressful, time-crunched, hasty, and often thoughtless approach to learning and living. This is the perplexing paradox of our culture; we are driven toward excellence and yet crippled by the process. Our current educational practices involve a focus on core competencies, but these competencies are academically based; they ignore the other psychological aspects (needs) that are required to be learned optimally, which help us adapt to the ever-changing world.

Certainly we need to learn to read, write, think scientifically, and be competent with mathematics (actually much more competent than most of our students are currently)! Certainly these subjects are critical. However, these "non-academic" skills, also are the "essence"-tial attitudes, skills, and knowledge and are disconnected from our current curriculum requirements. Although the interventions are well founded in research and in some cases practiced over thousands of years, these approaches are not usually incorporated into our educational process or not incorporated in an efficient manner.

This strange paradox for our fast-paced culture and the need to slow down is more than a little bit puzzling. It is downright threatening to the development of our children, of self, and our society, not only for the short term, but also over the life span and beyond, as similar patterns tend to repeat. Thus, the lifetime of our grandchildren and so forth are impacted. Furthermore, this paradox results in many disconnects between what and how children are prepared for life.

Looking closer at the paradoxes and disconnects and trying to understand the phenomena involved are the next steps to bridging the gaps educationally. Discovering what underlies these quirks and chasms requires a look at how research and other aspects of our country work and putting forth the right questions. For example, are these preventing us from optimal learning and preparation for managing life as a result of

- Being too stressed out? Or not being under enough stress to understand the importance of education?
- Being forced to grow up too quickly? Or being overprotected by helicopter parents?
- Being pulled in to many directions? Or being in a society that is overly specialized?
- Being out of balance? Or being overly conscious of homeostasis and fearful of change?
- Being bombarded by so many options and approaches? Or being distrustful of the ways of others?
- Being a matter of money as so many issues are ... bottom line? Or is there enough money not well managed?
- Being a matter of who has the loudest voice and the most clout politically?

Well, it probably has to do with each of these factors and more. Understanding some of the disconnects may well help us understand the way to intervene.

DISCONNECT BETWEEN RESEARCH AND APPLICATION

As we learned in chapter 1, researchers and academics, including J.D. Bransford and members from the Committee on Developments in the Science of

Learning and Committee on Learning Research and Educational Practice, Commission on Behavioral and Social Sciences and Education, and National Research Council, have documented their findings in *How People Learn: Brain, Mind, Experience, and School* (Washington, DC: National Academy Press). Even as far back as the 1980s, they have mentioned the disconnect between research and application. At the time, they were referring to research conducted during the 1960s and earlier, which was not well applied educationally. (In Bransford, 2004)

This well-acknowledged disconnect has been blamed on many practices in the past, including the researchers being stuck in their ivy towers and not really knowing what was going on the classroom. Nonetheless, what becomes clear from this work and earlier works upon which the current work is based is that the very problem still exists, and there indeed is little, systematic, comprehensive research applied in our schools. Despite the suggestions made to combine the efforts of the researchers with the wisdom of classroom professionals.

Over the past decade or more, tremendous strides have been made in the fields of medicine, technology, and psychology in understanding and learning and the brain, but the repetition of a lack of appropriate application persists, and the puzzle of the disconnect between research and practice remains problematic. We have become so highly specialized in our areas of practices with a tremendous need for collaboration and interdisciplinary work.

DISCONNECT BETWEEN RESEARCH METHODOLOGIES

Furthermore, there is even a disconnect between theory and research. Scientific, including psychological, theories have been developed from scientific research. Earlier forms of research included observation and case studies which can be a good starting point, but then those must be replicated repeatedly using various methodologies. Qualitative methodologies are still very important as they can yield in-depth insight into an individual's experiential life, which is crucial to understanding very essential or emotional aspects of a person.

As usual we are seeing the problem with our fast-paced research-focused nation. Research too is fast paced and new information is being discovered daily as we are able to better view the brain and its functioning, but it requires time and replication.

There has been a movement away from (a disconnect) such studies because of the difficulty in studying and quantifying the phenomenological aspects of an individual's being. This is similar to the strong focus on the academic subjects, while almost ignoring the more crucial psychological attitudes, behaviors, and emotions because these are more difficult to assess.

DISCONNECT BETWEEN FORMAL SCHOOLING AND PREPARING CHILDREN TO LEARN AND HANDLE LIFE'S CHALLENGES

It becomes clear that part of the problem lies with the fact that educational institutions are notorious for being the slowest to make changes, an interesting paradox in our fast-paced culture. But it is important to understand that slowness is not the entire problem, and that sometimes it can be helpful. Taking time, reflecting, and panning are all necessary parts for the development of well-prepared, educated, and thriving people.

However, one issue involves the fact that formal educational practices often ignore the psychological aspects of a child's readiness for learning and may actually be teaching children to disconnect from their whole selves or to be incongruent. Young children are often expected to put their emotions aside to address the academic tasks. Children experiencing problems at home or at school are expected to be able to put these issues on hold during school hours, a most unrealistic expectation for children and even most adults.

Of course, from research and from our own experiences as a child and working with children, we know that children experience intense emotions, which often go unidentified because they have not learned to name and use their emotions effectively. This is an area we do not deal with in our schools, yet recent research in neuroscience clearly indicates the important role that affect has on learning. Being ready to learn means being able to identify and work with one's emotions. It is almost as if there is a required splitting of the child from his/her emotions, thoughts, and behaviors.

Such incongruence is not healthy and according to Goleman (2008): "Curiosity, risk-taking, questioning, experimentation are largely written out of classroom conversations. Failure is feared rather than learned from; aggressive competition becomes the mode for rising above one's peers; reward and incentives are dispensed to the lucky few whose minds match the medium." (In Eckman, 2008, p.ix) He goes on to assert that Howard Gardner's emotional intelligence is more important than aptitude and involves the development of commitment, discipline restraint, and ambition. Furthermore, it is these very same abilities that are essential for sustained lifelong learning.

Moreover, most healthy young children are full of energy: physically needing to move around, creatively needing an outlet for the expression of their ideas, and so forth. Instead these basic attributes are often squelched, and the child begins to believe that these needs are somehow wrong or even bad.

DISCONNECT BETWEEN TEACHER PREPARATION AND THE TEACHER'S PROFESSIONAL NEEDS

Another area that needs mentioning is the gap between the needed knowledge and skills required of teachers. Teachers have gone through the same traditional schooling that has neglected their psychological development as well. Indeed, all of us have not been nurtured in a manner that prepares us well to handle life's challenges; thus, it is like the blind leading the blind. Our teacher preparation programs should be considerably updated as mentioned in previous books, including *Hidden Dangers*, *Global Education*, and *Barriers to Excellence* (In Eckman, 2008, p. ix) (Gunzelmann,2008; 2012; 2014).

The psychological preparation required to teach (to be successful at arguably the most important job on this planet) is an area that is not addressed in current teacher preparation programs. Young teachers are sent out on a wing and a prayer, hoping that they have developed the emotional, cognitive, and behavioral skills along with the required knowledge to help our children develop these necessary attributes for learning readiness, but many have not yet developed these skills themselves.

THE STRANGE DISCONNECT WITH THE NEEDS OF LIFE

Strangely enough there are major disconnects between what is being taught in our schools and what is needed to thrive out in the world. Having observed first hand how students graduating from high school and beginning the college years have not been prepared to be independent learners, capable of managing their time, emotions, or other aspects are not ready to take on the challenges of higher education. According to Ben Locke from Penn State (2015 report by the Center for Collegiate Mental Health) there are very clear and concerning trends that indicate that college student mental health is declining, not improving. Thus students are less ready for learning, ready for life.

Moreover, by looking closer at the needs of the younger generations going out into the world of work whether upon completion of high school or higher education, it is evident that most of these young adults have little grounding in handling finances, responsibilities, or other coming-of-age requirements. This whole ready-for-learning, ready-for-life approach is a process that needs to begin as early in childhood as possible, yet we should not be pessimistic with starting where we are at; it is never too late.

Likewise, this disconcerting disconnect persists to haunt us throughout our lifetime.

Sarah Lawrence Lightfoot (2009) asserts: "What is fascinating—and disturbing—about most of the public discourse, policies, and educational practices is there is seldom a reference to the longitudinal trajectory of learning across the lifespan. For the most part, school learning does not anticipate or help students prepare for lifelong learning. The goals of schooling tend to be shortsighted and narrowly pragmatic" (pp. 235–36).

Learning is a lifelong process. It is not something that just occurred during the school-aged years. Lightfoot wrote of the difficulties she witnessed when interviewing forty subjects for her research, with older adults confronting a major life transition, for they were not well prepared by our traditional educational experience. Lightfoot (2009) states:

> "Several people spoke of having to undo the long-entrenched habits, values and norms in school life in order to embrace the challenges. ..." The very aptitudes and attitudes ... seemed to be barriers to the risk-taking and adventuresomeness that allowed them to embark on new learning. (p. 234)

DISCONNECT BETWEEN VALUES AND POLICIES

The ultimate disturbing disconnect is the schism between what we say are our values and our practices; in plain and simple terms, it is putting our money where our mouths are. It is not just the responsibility of the child, the parents, the teachers, administrators, or policy makers, but it requires an integrative process where everybody is involved to create and maintain a healthy approach and climate where one can learn, grow, and be ready for life's challenges.

The societal conflicts, politics, and misinformation contribute to this serious impediment to helping our children become ready for learning and ready for life. This book will help clear up the misinformation and the disconnects and will allow us to fully address the preparation needs of our children, for learning and for a lifetime.

As we will see in the upcoming chapters, this process in many ways is ancient and in other ways involves cutting-edge interdisciplinary research from related sciences, along with an integration of the arts and philosophy.

Chapter 3

Catalysts to Our Understanding
Theoretical and Research Foundations

What humans can be, they must be. They must be true to their own nature.

—Abraham H. Maslow

Building a strong foundation is essential for healthy psychological development to ensure readiness for learning and readiness for life. Thus, this chapter begins with a review of the relevant psychological theories pertaining to understanding the needs for a readiness for life, which begins with the development of self.

Erik Erickson's psychosocial theory seems a good place to begin. Erikson used case-study research to formulate his theory. He was trained in the psychoanalytic tradition, but differed from the Freudian concepts believing that the social aspects of development were more important than the psychosexual stages of Freud's theory.

In addition, Erikson's theory goes throughout the life span which is a much more useful framework to help us understand the varying issues and needs that arise requiring different needs and abilities to cope with learning—which a lifelong process.

According to Erikson's theory, the individual is faced with a crisis that he or she must cope with, resulting in either an adaptive or a maladaptive manner. Erikson used the term "crisis" to mean an encounter or conflict with the environment and involves a change in perspective. (When a conflict is not successfully resolved it is more difficult, but still possible to achieve a successful outcome.) The individual can develop basic strengths that are motivating characteristics or beliefs derived from the satisfactory resolution of a crisis at each developmental level.

One should realize that no one has a perfect resolution at each stage. It is more a result of issues, situations, and events that occur, making each of us unique in our psychosocial development.

The stages are as follows:

Erikson called the first stage as the oral-sensory stage (from birth to approximately age 1). At this time, the child learns through his or her sense of touch. As you are probably aware, infants need constant supervision because everything tends to go into their mouths, but with guidance they can learn, ideally learning to trust their caregivers and environment and thus developing the strength of hope that keeps them moving forward on the path to healthy development.

Muscular-anal (approximately from age 1 to 3), if negotiated well, is the next stage where the child can learn to become more autonomous and develop the strength of will. In this stage, he or she becomes motivated and more self-determined or unfortunately may learn to be shameful and self-doubting. Naturally, there are many things going on with a child of this age, but centrally he or she learns to use words and be quite mobile!

Erikson termed the third stage occurring approximately at age 3–5 as the muscular-genital stage. Children become much more active and coordinated, quite verbal, and aware of gender differences. If this stage is adaptively negotiated, the child develops a sense of initiative, where he or she believes in his or her capabilities and develops a strength of purpose. Maladaptive coping may result in feelings of guilt and and a lack of confidence (Schultz & Schultz, 2013). Most children start attending school at the preschool to kindergarten levels during this age. How the child progresses has much to do with his or her early introduction to school, peers, teachers, and so forth.

At age 6–11, formal schooling is well underway, and it is the central "job" for the child. If he or she does not feel successful for whatever the reasons, then the child may develop inferiority feeling. On the other hand, during this latency stage children can develop strong coping skills of industriousness and strong competency.

During the adolescent years (age 12–18), the youth focuses on his or her identity and really begins to develop an understanding of who he or she really is, or they may be quite confused—It should be noted that in Western society, oftentimes this stage goes well into the 20s+ because students have the luxury of taking their time to choose their careers, going on to graduate school, and so forth. Of course, many of the career paths are much more complex and did not even exist when Erikson developed this theory. However, Erikson himself had several "identity crisis" and really did not find his "niche" until his late 20s (Schultz & Schultz, 2013).

Then we have students transitioning (for which they are so poorly prepared) into college, living away from home, into the military, or into the world of work. It is no wonder that so many psychological disorders tend to emerge at this highly stressful stage. Erikson dubbed this stage "young adulthood" where issues of intimacy and love or feelings of isolation come into play (Schultz & Schultz, 2013). Clearly, the feelings of friendship and belonging are essential at the much earlier stages as well. Certainly, many children have difficulty making friends at earlier stages, and such issues of isolation can have serious consequences and reoccur throughout one's life. Maslow's theory, discussed later in this chapter, will help us understand this.

In our society, many young people tend to hurry to get into relationships or get married even before establishing their identity, which is often not in their best interest. The results of such behavior is evidenced through very high divorce rates.

Middle years (ages between 33 and 55, which vary in today's society) are fraught with settling down roots, climbing the corporate ladder, dealing with aging parents and growing children, and so forth (Schultz & Schultz, 2013). Adulthood is the stage where individuals adapt to aging process by "giving back" to the younger generation and obtaining a sense of caring, or if maladaptive, developing a sense of stagnation or being caught up in the treadmill of life. It is at this stage that many people might decide to give up lucrative careers in order to give back to the younger cohorts by teaching and thereby developing a feeling of integrity and purpose.

Erikson termed the older years, aged 55 and above—this is greatly extended in today's society since many are living well into their 90s and move forward to 100 and above—as the maturity-old stage. In this stage people could find ego integrity and a strength of wisdom or a sense of despair (Schultz & Schultz, 2013).

Early Americans worked hard and long and died at young age unable to retire. As our country started prospering, people were beginning to live longer through advances in medicine, and many were able to look forward to rest and relaxation in their later years. Now we are seeing a different trend developing where the retirement years may span 30+ years. Many older people do not want to sit and do nothing, but to continue to feel a sense of purpose, to produce and contribute.

We are who we are because of how we have negotiated these stages. Whatever stage, if we are/were fortunate, things worked out well and we thrived. Erikson's theory does suggest that people can overcome a difficult beginning, but it does not delve is that each one of us has faced specific circumstances and might have perceived situations quite differently; therefore, we think, feel, and behave differently. However, by Erikson's theory as the foundation, we will see how this can help guide us toward being ready for learning and ready to face today's life challenges with the integration of current research.

Alfred Adler's theory can offer insight into the needs of individuals and their development. He believed that all of us have inferiority feelings (to some degree); however, these feelings can motivate us to improve. On the more extreme end, when students are unable to compensate for normal inferiority feelings, they develop inferiority complex, which is an unhealthy aspects. This results in the person being out of balance or incongruent and one who tries to strive for superiority. Such people may feel a false sense of confidence and may be belittled by others over work at the expense of self. This theory offers hope by pointing out that the individual creates himself or herself, and their style of life and personality. The implication is that we can intervene!

Jungian theory also offers insight into an aspect of psychological development that so many shy away from in research, and that of the spiritual aspects of the individual. Carl Jung sums up how this aspect relates to learning and life: "One looks back with appreciation to the brilliant teachers, but with gratitude to those who touched our human feelings. The curriculum is so much necessary raw material, but warmth is the vital element for the growing plant and for the soul of the child."

Jung analytic theory involves a concept of synchronicity that helps bridge between the deterministic theories such as Freud's, where he believed people are determined by their past and the humanistic and existential theorists who believe strongly in free will and a sense of purpose (Boeree, 2006). This is a useful concept since each child is influenced by his or her genetic makeup, as well as environmental and social factors. This of course makes sense, but the synchronicity comes into play because of our free will to make choices, to strive to make changes, and to strive toward one's potential.

Carl Rogers, a humanistic psychologist, worked with individuals who were experiencing psychological problems, but his theory focused on elements that contribute to becoming a fully functioning person. These psychologically healthy characteristics include creativity, an awareness of experience and open to both positive and negative feelings, and confidence in one's feelings and behaviors, along with a continual need to grow. Rogers discusses the need for congruence with aspects of one's life. (Congruence implies the individual's thoughts, feelings, and behaviors are not in conflict.)

However, when an individual is not emotionally healthy, experiencing incongruencies, he or she becomes vulnerable, anxious, depressed, and self-doubting. He or she develops low self-esteem and incongruencies in self-perception (In Schultz & Schultz, 2013). Such lower functioning people are not well prepared for learning or for coping with life's conflicts.

Maslow's theory of needs to becoming a self-actualizing (healthy) individual can help us understand the basic needs of people to move toward growth. His focus on human strengths, aspirations, conscious free will, and a need to fulfill one's potential can help us bridge the gap between theory and research to help all children (and adults) live fully. Back in 1971, Abraham Maslow suggested that psychology needed to integrate the whole person: body, mind, and spirit.

This theory begins at the base of a pyramid image, with human physiological needs being the most basic needs that must be satisfied. For example, we must have food, water, and air to survive. Likewise, when we can breathe and move from at least a minimal amount of water and nourishment, our safety needs become paramount. Children who live in drug-riddled neighborhoods or are abused have their basic safety needs violated. It is difficult, if not impossible, to think about academic subjects when these essentials are not met.

The next level is where psychological needs become active. These include the need to feel as sense of belonging and love, a sense of community, and avoiding isolation or alienation. Then comes esteem needs, which involve self-esteem through achievement, competence, and independence. Esteem needs also come from receiving earned recognition and respect from others. Esteem needs must be real or earned, or the individual will not develop real self-esteem as researcher Stanley Coppersmith (1960) found.

Ideally next comes the level of self-actualization, which involves living up to one's fullest potential. Certainly not everyone reaches this level, nor do individuals who, according to Maslow's theory, function at the highest level continually to achieve this level. I like to look at this self-actualized level as one that includes fulfilling one's purpose in an engaged healthy way.

It should be noted that a lower level need may not always be fully met before a higher need kicks in, but it should be clear that basics such as nourishment, shelter, and safety make it very difficult to worry about learning geometry. Maslow saw the lower level needs as being deficit needs. When a person failed to meet these needs, a deficit in the body would occur. When higher development is foiled, pathologies may occur. On the other hand, the higher-level needs are growth needs that help us realize our full potential.

Maslow also developed a second set of innate needs separate from the previous pyramid. These cognitive needs involve the need to know and understand, and are necessary to become self-actualized. These involve the natural curiosity of the person—often thwarted by traditional schooling due to core curriculum, high-stakes testing, unreasonable rules for sitting still, and not exploring one's environment—for a quest or thirst for knowledge. These innate needs to begin late in the infancy stage (possibly before) and in the early childhood period.

Innate needs involve cognition and lead us right into an understanding of Piaget's theory of cognitive development. Piaget also based his theory upon case studies subsequently and has been one of the most widely researched theories to date. More recent findings indicate that all children seem to go through these cognitive stages but some may reach stages earlier than Piaget found. The early stages from birth to about 2 years of age involve sensory-motor learning, through touch and movement. (One might note that even at older ages, when something is very new, we may need to pick it up, look at it, and experience it to fully understand. So, our senses and behavior (motor movement) play a significant role in later learning as well.)

In the 2 to 6-year-old stage, language develops and plays an important role in learning. It is a sort of experiential role-play approach to learning. However, children of this age are still unable to think logically. Logic comes into play only during ages 7–11, and children develop the ability to manipulate mathematical operations. Moral reasoning and the ability to think in a "what if" abstract manner of thought develop during ages of 12 to adulthood for most people exposed to schooling.

According to Piaget, it is essential to understand that children need to be ready to handle content, and young children do not think in the same manner as older children, or even those who have had exposure to scientific thinking. The foundation or scaffolding of learning is important. For example, one needs to learn that anything with four legs is not always a dog. When foundations are strong, the sky may not be the limit.

Lev Vygotsky, a Russian psychologist, added to Piaget's theory by showing how one's culture and interaction with others play a significant role in cognitive development. Furthermore, children have *windows of opportunity* when they are exposed to certain subjects and concepts for optimal learning.

A behavioral theorist can also help us understand how and why we perform certain actions. The definition for learning, as a change in thinking, feeling and behaving is a good starting point. The behaviorists focused on measureable, quantifiable stimuli and the resulting responses, and observable behavior. This was a movement away from the qualitative research of many previous theorists who used mostly case studies to develop their theories.

Behavioral research could be conducted following experimental methodology, which was embraced by the medical and other scientific fields. The problem with the psychology of people is that both qualitative and quantitative approaches are needed to delve deep to explain the complexities and uniqueness of an individual.

B. F. Skinner contributed significantly on the uses of reinforcement and the schedules of reinforcement to increase behaviors with his research with pigeons and rats (Schultz & Schultz, 2013). Yet, although important, his research is lacking since the human condition involves higher level thinking.

Albert Bandura's social learning theory helps illustrate the powerful role that observational learning plays with humans (and even animals). His term "reciprocal determinism" explains the behavior that involves as an interaction between environmental events and individual factors (motivation and cognition). The crux of the research suggests that people can observe and learn antisocial behaviors or positive, constructive, helpful behaviors (Schultz & Schultz, 2013). It is our job to provide the healthy models.

The early work on achievement motivation by David McClelland focused on a more specific aspect of an individual's personality. He defined it as "the need or desire to do things well, overcome obstacles, to do things better." He also identified that people high in achievement motivation like a challenge usually do not take on a task that is way over the ability level. These individuals will take calculated risks but are not gamblers; they are not rewarded so much by external reinforcers of money or praise as they would be by internal sources of excitement over their accomplished goal. Motivation can be a more important factor to achieve high grades than intelligence alone. Furthermore, McClelland believed that such achievement motivation could be encouraged or even taught. could be taught (Schultz & Schultz, 2013 and http://www.accel-team.com/human_relations/hrels_06_mcclelland.html).

From the thought-provoking research of Martin Seligman (1990; 1996; 1997; 1998; 2011), we know that schools can and should teach and project optimism. He and his colleagues continued to research in the field positive psychology, yielding continued support to his findings. Seligman clearly emphasized that failure can occur in the school even with very talented and motivated students (and teachers) if there is a pessimistic perspective. Therefore, an optimistic attitude is necessary, which can be learned and nurtured.

It involves seeing how we perceive situations. For example, how might a student explain his or her failure in a math exam? Is it because of a belief that he or she is incapable of learning any subject or could learn if he or she tried? Thus, is it global or specific to one subject and does he or she explain the grade in terms that can be modified, and does not threaten his or her core being? Is it explained as a permanent or temporary situation that can get better?

Seligman also discusses the concept of "learned helplessness," which is a condition of human depression, an illness afflicting so many within our culture (1990; 1996; 1997; 1998; 2011). In a nutshell, learned helplessness can develop when situations or events occur. This can develop into problematic behavior if the individual perceives there is nothing he or she can do to change the situation or cope with the event. Under such circumstances, many give up trying and learn to be helpless. Children and adults need to learn better ways of coping with learning and life transitions.

All of these foundational theories have helped pave the way for our current understanding, and specific cutting-edge research methods have been applied in a unique manner that addresses the needs for the children (indeed all of us) to become ready for learning and ready for life. These will be discussed in the upcoming chapters. I have attempted to systematically analysis the research and experiences of others in a manner that attempts to help close the disconnects we are seeing (as discussed in chapter 2). Some of the grounded theory information is from previous research as well as from those of others as referenced within the text.

In addition, I have used a meta-analytic approach to further assist with building the framework to theory and practice. This method is well explained by Card (2012), who states: "Meta-analysis, also called quantitative research synthesis, is a powerful way of summarizing and comparing empirical results and is often used in the social sciences." (p. 3) Over the next several chapters, we shall see the results of this analysis more specifically and suggestions for application.

Chapter 4

A Current Understanding of the Development of Readiness

What usually happens in the educational process is that the faculties are dulled, overloaded, stuffed and paralyzed so that by the time most people are mature they have lost their innate capabilities.

—R. Buckminster Fuller

Understanding the paradoxes and disconnects is important, but so is moving on to the next steps of understanding what it means to be ready for learning and ready for life. Getting ready for learning and ready for life does not imply a time schedule, start and finish lines, or a race to be first. It does not imply becoming "someone else" as a way of coming of age. On the other hand, it implies getting all the "gears" working together (sort to speak) to become more fully the person you were meant to be, not have our faculties diminished.

Thus, it means developing a way of being, that is, a *synergistic process* that can be taught and nurtured within each child to indeed be ready for learning and ready for life. It imparts ways of thinking, feeling, and behaving that allow each of us to cope with the realities of our environment and our circumstances, and thrive or rise above these factors.

Now that we have had a solid foundation of the aspects of the individual's personality and development that are intricately involved with learning and life, we can move on to clarify how these elements interact in a synergistic manner, which is unique to each person. In figure 4.1, we can see that there are internal influences on each person that involve our genetic/biological makeup, and overall physical and psychological development.

According to Chopra and Tanzi (2012) our brains basically bridge to the aspects of our biology and experience; one without the other is an inadequate explanation.Furthermore, looking just from a biological perspective suggests we cannot change. We now know that nothing could be further from the truth, since our mind is the product of the interaction of these aspects.

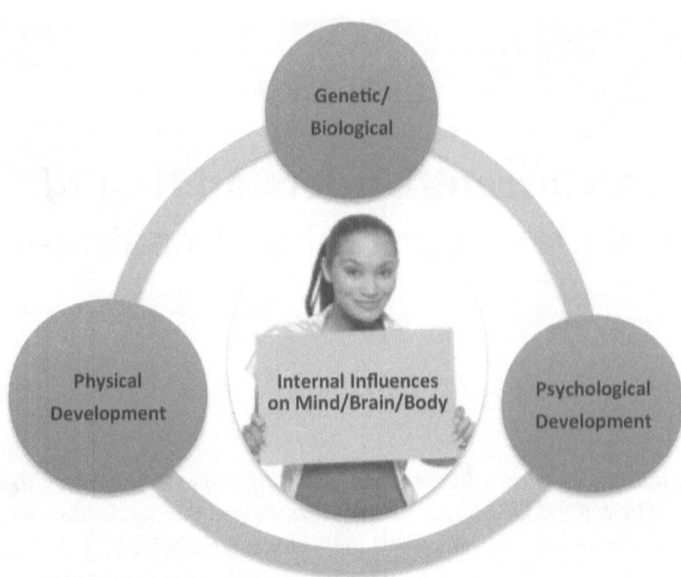

Figure 4.1 The Synergistic Process.

Thus, we (our mind/brain/body connection) are influenced by our genetic/biological/physical makeup and our environment, which result in a unique cognitive, emotional, behavioral, and physical development. There is a much overlapping interaction with each aspect. Furthermore, at times there may be factors that inhibit growth, while other factors may enhance growth.

The schools, parents, pediatricians, and those involved with the healthy development of children usually do a great job by addressing the above areas. However, my concern is the lack of attention to the psychological elements, which can be further broken down to include physical, cognitive, emotional, spiritual, and behavioral properties.

Figure 4.2 breaks down these elements into distinct parts for clarity. However, it should be understood that each of these processes involves an interaction with the whole body. For example, although the psychological aspects of a person are not visible since we do not have concrete places within the body that deal with emotions or one's spirit, we can diagram these as separately just as we talk about our mind or immune system, which involves complex interactions within the brain and body.

It may seem obvious to the reader that the mind, the brain, and the body are all connected, and in fact there is no organ called the "mind." When we think of the mind, we tend to think of our brains. But our minds are really much more than just this very the essence of self-hood, and there may be an element of the mind involving the psychological processing of our whole selves.

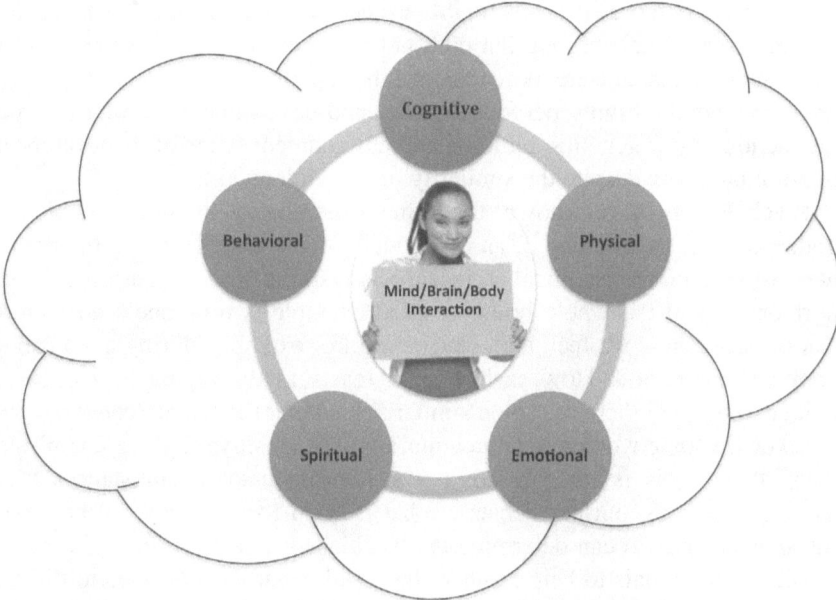

Figure 4.2 One Mind/One Brain/One Body and Environment.

The brain is the physical organ that interacts with the body and the nervous system in amazing ways, ways in which we are finally able to understand, view, measure, that is, in "mind-blowing" ways. However, what is really mind blowing (pun intended) is that we cannot actually see, touch, or measure the mind. Thus, for clarity, these internal influences result in each person's unique psychology, our unique mind set. Of course, the processes are not discrete, but occur in a connected fashion. (see figure 4.2)

Then the manner in which each person interacts with his or her environment is also essential to assisting with developing readiness for learning and for life. Although the environmental factors definitely compound the interactions, they also allow for many more ways to interact and intervene with each individual.

The cloud in the background of figure 4.2 depicts the individual's interaction with his or her environment.

The psychological elements: We then have the psychological aspects of the individual. Naturally not each element is totally distinct from the other, and the physical aspects overlap greatly with the psychological elements as well. Nonetheless, I term the psychological elements as those that deal with one's cognitions (thoughts, beliefs, and attitudes), one's emotions, one's core essence or sense of self, and one's behaviors (the result of these prior psychological aspects).

The mind is more of an intangible aspect of our humanness; some may say an abstract concept, but that does not really exist. But it is important to understand that people are more than just the sum of their individual parts; we are more than our brains, nervous systems, and flesh and bones; we are a true interaction of our genetics, biology, and environment. Each of us develops a mind of our own, despite the similarity of our biological makeup.

Psychologists have known for some time that it is not possible to understand the psychology of an individual without understanding the brain, nervous system, the chemical and electrical activities (neurotransmitters and hormones), and the whole body. A good example is how one's hormones can influence how we feel, and what we do, for example, during a woman's premenstrual period. How each woman reacts to the raging hormones is unique to her, yet there are some similarities among the female gender.

Likewise some women are much more highly sensitive to these chemicals than others. This is true also of one's environmental circumstances (the age-old nature vs. nurture debate). What is good for one may not be good for another, but we can determine the basic needs and learn from the more sensitive individuals to help provide them with what they do need to thrive. Thus, in psychology we understand the mind to be the totality of what the brain thinks, perceives, and does.

The medical field is coming back around to the importance of this mind-body connection. Although medical doctors too have always known that we are all connected, understanding the dynamics of these interactions has been so elusive that research focused more on the tangible, measureable features. The medical field realizes the "powerful mind-body connection through which emotional, mental, social, spiritual, and behavioral factors can directly affect our health." (NLM.NIH 2008, p. 4)

Furthermore, there are multiple dynamic interactions with one's environment that play key roles in this readiness. The individual does not operate without stimuli from the outside, from one's environment. Figure 4.2 breaks down these influences that have a direct bearing upon the individual. Even the country and culture that one is a part of has significant influence upon the individual's environment, including the politics and policymakers for our schools, for example. The cloud in the background of figure 4.3 depicts these broader influences.

When all is in harmony, the individual is able to function optimally. This brings us to the question, "How do we get the individual synchronized to be ready for learning and ready for life?" Clearly this is not totally answerable, given our current level of understanding, but there are many ways to help develop the needed synchronicity.

Each area is expressed by the individual through a complex interaction/synergy with all factors. For example, how we think is influenced by our genetic, biological, and psychological dimensions interacting with our external factors of environment issues and expressed cognitively through our thoughts, ideas, and beliefs. In turn each thought influences how we feel, behave, and our basic essence of who we are, that is, our self-concept. Likewise, what we eat, how much we exercise, and so forth influences how we feel, think, and behave.

The task is to maximize the individual's strengths and minimize his or her weaknesses by promoting interventions that work. Well this seems like a "duh" statement if I have ever heard one. Psychologists have known for decades the importance of in education how much we understand the students strength and weaknesses. But so often what happens is that students are taught to their strengths, and weaknesses remain weaknesses; synchronicity cannot develop with such an approach. We will see greater imbalance and dysfunction.

What is needed are approaches that awaken the whole person, allowing for the development of weak areas as well; setting up an optimal readiness for learning.

Sounds good in theory, but the reality is that this is not a science fiction. Helping students learn in this manner is grounded upon solid research-based interventions. The problem is that these interventions have never been

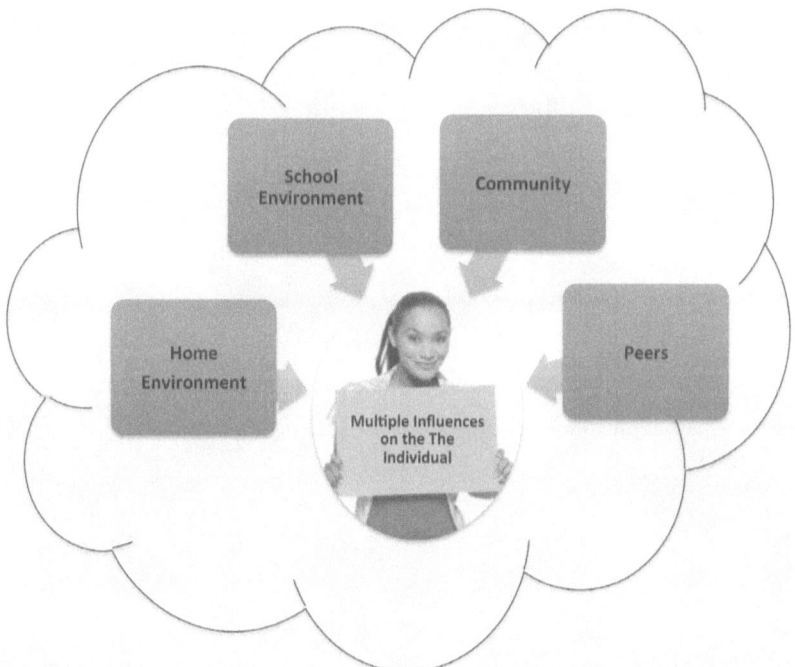

Figure 4.3 Multiple Influences on the Individual.

implemented on large scales, or consistently for all of the reasons we went over in chapter 2 on the paradoxes and disconnects!

Consequently, analyzing well research-based approaches that can indeed awaken the whole person and helps develop strengths and reduce weaknesses. Getting the interaction of the mind/brain and body working in harmony with one's environment is the next task at hand. Thus, in the next several chapters, I will be breaking down each of the individual facets of physical, cognitive, emotional, and spiritual along with specific addresses of the environmental concerns.

This is not a trial to reinvent the wheel, but merely an attempt to help bridge the disconnects and confront the paradoxes that exists within our educational system that our children to be ready for learning and ready for life.

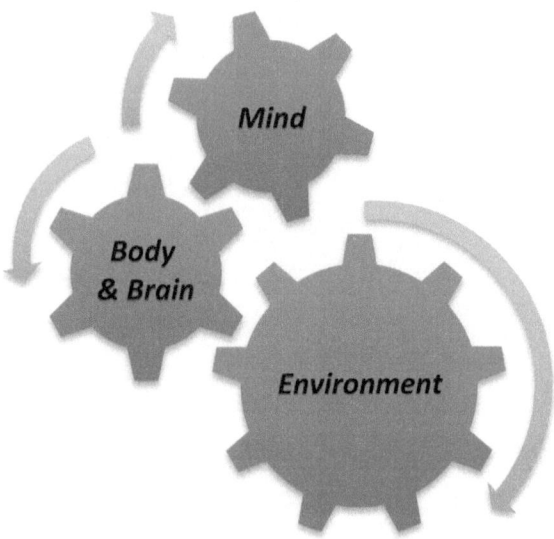

Figure 4.4 Synergistic Process.

Part II

THE SYNERGISTIC READINESS

Kids go to school and college and get through, but they don't seem to really care about using their minds. School doesn't have the kind of long term positive impact that it should.

—Howard Gardner

So our working definition of being ready for learning and ultimately to become ready for life appears to require a synergistic process of one's brain/mind/body working in harmony with the environment in a manner that requires openness to new experiences, and is growth oriented.

The next several chapters will break these areas down for straightforwardness to show how previously well-researched approaches can indeed awaken facets within the individual to allow for a readiness for learning. The internal and external influences are expressed through an interaction between the unique physical, cognitive, emotional, behavioral, and spiritual development of the individual.

Chapter 5

The Physical Piece

Physiological traits in themselves do not necessarily limit or define a child's potential.

—Brazelton & Greenspan, 2000, p. 83

The physical elements can help or hinder the readiness for learning and the readiness for life. Of course, we have no control over some of our physical development such as our genetic makeup and physical limitations. Yet, new research indicates that we have more control over some aspects than originally thought to help us optimize our readiness. Indeed, there is much we can do to promote a healthy physical development.

All parents should regularly consult with their primary care physician for checkups and advice. With that notification established, the information presented here looks at development from the perspective of a psychologist with knowledge in human growth and development and related fields.

Many assume that human physical development begins at conception. Although others might argue that each of our developmental paths began much earlier, linking our parents and previous ancestors with how their genetics played out in their lives. The important message here is that we need to be aware of how we take care of our children and ourselves may have much farther-reaching impacts than originally thought. .

So let's begin this discussion with a basic definition of physical development which refers to the biological changes that occur within an individual. The genetic makeup of the person is orchestrated throughout the processes of physical growth, motor movement skills, as well as the chemical and electrical interactions within the body and brain. Thus, these physical progressions are interconnected with brain development, sensation, perception learning, and overall well-being of the person, which in turn influences how we think (cognitive), feel (emotional), react (behavioral, and our very core (spiritual). Clearly the distinction made here is only for purposes of clarification.

Physical development is a complex interaction that results in the whole person (and all aspects of the self) being much greater than the sum of these parts. Indeed, it is the development of these differences over time (along with the interaction with the environment) that makes us unique with varying abilities and readiness to learn and apply learned information to handle life's encounters. Our mind/brain/body connection, the expression of hormones, neurotransmitters, and electrical activity within our systems are influenced by our genetic makeup and our environment which result in unique cognitive, emotional, behavioral, and physical development. There is much overlapping interaction with each aspect. At times, there may be factors that inhibit growth, while other factors may enhance growth.

We are developing insight into one of the biggest questions still unanswered in psychology: the age-old nature versus nurture debate. Research to date indicate that both are quite important and unique to each individual and require an ongoing process to unravel the complexities of this interaction, as well as which interventions might be most helpful, but there is significant research available to ascertain healthy options to enhance physical development.

Although approaches such as genetic engineering, to actually alter the genetic makeup of an individual when disorders arise, is becoming a reality, there are numerous ethical considerations involved and certainly beyond the scope of this research. My work involves a compilation of research studies that modify in ways that enhance the individual, as we shall see throughout the remainder of this book.

Essentially, for the healthy physical development of an individual, air, healthy nourishment, shelter, adequate sleep, and exercise are necessary. These essentials help the individual become ready for learning and ready for life. But even these essentials are not enough; each of us needs a sense of belonging and source of deep caring or love to thrive.

Air and nourishment: You might ask why I even bother to include these obvious life-sustaining necessities of air, food, and water. The reason is that many of our children do not receive adequate food or good air quality during the vitally important early years when the brain is making so many connections. As we know from chapter 2, these basic needs are at the foundational level of Maslow's hierarchy for survival needs, even more essential than higher-level needs, including learning.

Within the first two years of life, the myelin sheath develops around the axons to insulate and allows for conductivity between the neural connections. These connections allow learning to take place. Thus, the mother's diet during the pregnancy and the infant's diet are critical. Ideally, children will continue to be presented with healthy food options and regular medical visits to monitor their physical development.

Older children are not always under the constant supervision of their parents, though. When a child gets to school he or she is oftentimes presented with food choices that are not adequate nutritionally. Furthermore, each child's nutritional needs vary every day. Thus, healthy snacks and water, along with other nutritious options, should be readily available to children during school hours. Without adequate nourishment the brain will not function optimally, and children focus more on the lunch-hour bell than on their learning. Regular availability of nourishment allows children to develop a sense of eating when hungry and being tuned to their internal needs rather than eating because the clock tells us we should be hungry.

Healthy air conditions are critical. There are numerous environmental concerns about air quality in our communities and within our schools. I have researched and written about the air quality concerns and other environment hazards within our schools extensively in *Hidden Danger* and other publications. (Gunzelmann, 2008; 2010; 2011; 2013; 2015). Bad air quality in our schools and communities affects all of us, and difficulty in breathing is not a good footing for learning.

The most current asthma data provided by the CDC (2013) indicates that approximately 8.3% of children experience asthma with a sharp increase up to 9.9% among the 5 to 14-year-old schoolchildren, impacting more than 7 million children. Furthermore, between the years 2001 and 2011, the number of persons with asthma in the United States increased by 28%. (Cited in CDC. Asthma Facts: CDC's National Asthma Control Program Grantees.) Consequently, the CDC reports that children missed more than 10 million school days, (para. 4), not to mention the days they were in school but not fully functioning from either the illness itself or the side effects of medication.

Exercise/motor stimulation: Likewise, adequate exercise is essential for learning. Ratey and Manning (2014) asserted: "Our inactivity is making us dumber" (pp. 105, 107). On the other hand, exercise activates brain growth, enlarges hippocampal area, and prevents loss of gray matter (p. 107). Exercise can make us smarter and may help set the stage for learning.

Striving for optimal learning involves making the best use of our genetic inheritances and changing what we can to increase mental and physical well-being. Each of us need not be star athletes to balance this necessity for our brains and bodies. The word "balance" is used here to imply a peak level for well-being, not an end point as the word "homeostasis" can imply. Balance indicates that one is at a point, and that he or she can develop and reach higher levels; it allows for growth.

Exercise, the regular need to move around, is healthy for both our brains and bodies. Often children are required to sit still and stay in their seats which is counter (disconnected from) all solid research on child development, yet this is exactly the expectation within our schools! Furthermore, the ability to sit idle varies between the genders—many boys have a need to move around regularly—and from child to child. If we are sincere in our desire to help children become ready for learning, we should allow for more regular exercise, gym classes, and recess. These critical areas should not be cut from the curriculum, but included as a natural and fun way to stay focused and flourishing.

In addition to regularly scheduled exercise, many children may need to walk around and fidget, rather than sitting still. Exercise need not be presented as a chore to children either. In fact, it should be pleasant, fun, and social. Indeed, it should involve play at the young ages, and old ages for that matter. Sometimes we get caught up in the idea that if it's fun it's not work and we're not learning. Nothing could be further from the truth. Exercise is essential according to Ratey and Manning (2014), but they recommend out in wild real world where all aspects of our being are involved, not like just walking on a treadmill.

Sleep: Our bodies and brains also require adequate sleep in order to develop and function well. Without sleep, we would not survive. With adequate sleep, we are able to make better judgments, and memory improves as does overall health and well-being. Furthermore, our sleep requirements tend to vary with age. Infants sleep up to about 18 hours, preschool children need 11–12 hours, school-aged youth require at least 10 hours, teenagers require about 9–10 hours, and adults between 7 and 8 hours per day. (CDC, 2013, para. 1)

According to the National Institute of Health: "During sleep, your body is working to support healthy brain function and maintain your physical health. In children and teens, sleep also helps support growth and development."

The NIH report goes on to explain that the results of sleep deficiency not only affect the individual, but also affect the society to a great extent since many accidents are related to sleep deficiency as a causal factor. Moreover, a lack of sleep can decrease learning and problem-solving ability, attention span, decision-making, and creativity. It also increases risks to developing mental health concerns and problem behaviors as well as physical health problems including heart disease, stroke, high blood pressure, and obesity. (Retrieved 6/25/15 from http://www.nhlbi.nih.gov/health/health-topics/topics/sdd/why)

It is alarming that teens experience a high degree of sleep deprivation that complicates their complex development and learning challenges. As reported by the American Psychological Association: "Lack of sufficient sleep—a rampant problem among teens—appears to put adolescents at risk for cognitive and emotional difficulties, poor school performance, accidents and psychopathology, research suggests." (Carpenter, 2001, p. 42)

James Mass, a top sleep researcher from Cornell University, reports that the research clearly indicates the negative impact on the adolescent population. (In Carpenter, 2001) With the evidence so clear one might ask why has the knowledge not be implemented to help our children. Again, there is a disconnect between research and practice.

Ratey and Manning (2014) explain how we need to expand our current understanding of the complexity and interrelatedness of problems, including issues of obesity. Many people believe it is all about one's genes or how much we eat or little one exercises. Research indicates, however, that obesity also can be related to how much one sleeps or even bacteria! Similarly, they assert that mental health issues such as depression are related to diet and exercise as well as brain chemistry.

Likewise, our physical development is just one piece of our total quest toward readiness for learning and readiness for life. The next piece of the to be discussed is cognitive element.

Chapter 6

The Cognitive Piece

Children must be taught how to think, not what to think.

—Margaret Mead

The cognitive element includes the mental processes involved with thinking, sensation, perception, memory, understanding, and reasoning. It involves the intellectual aspects as opposed to the emotional facets. Yet the brain does not think without the assistance or interaction with the body and the environment. It uses all elements that it is able to access and process. It is the cognitive element that is so highly prized and focused upon in our educational settings, oftentimes at the exclusion of the other pieces, which creates a system that works without all the information.

It is the underlying position of becoming ready for learning that all pieces are accessible to the individual. Yet for the purpose of discussion, we will be taking a closer look at what is involved with the cognitive element as it relates to learning and preparation for life.

Interestingly, there is no one model of cognition. We have looked at a couple of models in an earlier chapter to include the foundation of Piaget and Vygotsky. But numerous other theories have developed since their time. Each theory should be seen as looking at the same issues from different perspectives and adding more to our complete understanding. Psychologists, neurologists, psychiatrists, and educators all study "learning" in differing venues, but with the same goal: to understand what is involved with cognition and grasping the individual differences in learning. Indeed, defining cognition is really an exercise in cognition!

SENSATION AND PERCEPTION

Although these two occur almost simultaneously within the individual, it helps to break the terms down for clarity. Thus, sensing is a process by which our sensory receptors and nervous system receive and represent stimulus energy. Perception is a process of organizing and interpreting sensory information enabling us to recognize meaningful objects and events (Myers, 2011).

Each person must be able to sense or detect stimuli from his or her environment and then perceive or discern information about the stimuli. Furthermore, an individual can sense and perceive information through visual, auditory, olfactory, taste, or touch. Some individuals may be more sensitive to stimuli through one modality than through another. Thus if one is blind, the visual modality will not sense information from the environment; however, other senses may be more sensitive as a result. For example, non-sighted people often have a high sensitivity to touch and thus can learn to read (a typically sighted activity) by using braille (Myers, 2011).

To complicate matters a bit more, each individual does not sense and perceive things in exactly the same manner. For example, the color blue may not look the same to me as it does to you! Color blindness is an example of such differences, in perception wich involves an inability to detect colors as most people can, due to differences in the rods and cones within their retinas. Here again we can see the interaction with the physical element.

In addition, some people are more receptive to stimulation depending up several factors, including the person's experiences, expectations, motivation, and fatigue level (Myers, 2011). Clearly, then what we sense and perceive has a great deal to do with the physical elements, including health, amount of sleep, and alertness.

THINKING, UNDERSTANDING, AND REASONING

The next level of cognitive processing involves how we think about what we have detected from our environment. How do we make sense of our senses and perceptions? This involves reasoning, which can influence how we feel (emotional element) and even what we do!

When a young child knows a dog has four legs and then is confronted with a cat, how does he learn that a cat has four legs too, but it is a different animal than a dog? Well the child must be able to understand and perceive specific differences between the two species and then think about these differences and add to the schema of information.

Furthermore, how we analyze or explain information to ourselves can be explained in an optimistic or pessimistic manner? For example, does a child experiencing difficulty learning to read (by sensing, perceiving and making sense of written (visual) symbols explain this difficulty to him/herself as a temporary bump in the road of learning, that is only with this one subject, and that he/she can do something to remedy the problem optimistic cognition).

Or does he or she think that it is a permanent (he or she will never learn to read), and that he or she is stupid and there is nothing that can be done (pessimistic thought process).

A pessimistic outlook is associated with poor health, lower achievement, and overall lowered well-being and longevity. The good news is there are interventions that can help the child (or any of use) to become more optimistic (which does not mean unrealistic). Readers may want to refer to the research of Martin Seligman, (1990; 1996; 1998; 2011). Seligman's work has been verified over the years and is even essential for understanding chronic medical conditions.

Ongoing research studies have indicated that how we interpret situations also has a dramatic impact on us right down to the level of our genes. (Chopra & Tanzi, 2015) The implication is that our genetic makeup is no longer seen as being set in stone. We can improve how we cope with life's problems, learning, and even our health through life style changes.

Our understanding and reasoning of information can also guide behavior. For now, suffice it to say that what is understood and analyzed at this level can help motivate the child into further deeper investigation (learning). Misunderstanding can result in less desirable behaviors, such as acting out, and in extreme cases mental illness.

MEMORY

The level of physical preparedness can influences how well a child is able to negotiate these cognitive tasks. A good working definition of memory is given by Myers, to involve the persistence of learning over time through the storage and retrieval of information. People have short-term memory, for example, remembering information such as a phone number or street address. Such pieces of information are remembered as long as they are needed and are discarded when no longer needed. Long-term memory stores information (in various places within the brain) with relatively limitless storage capacity (Myers, 2011).

Memory is also dependent upon several physical factors. For example, how alert the individual is (physical illness, fatigue, and hunger or thirst) could definitely negatively influence the encoding of information.

Information is encoded visually, auditorally, or semantically. Furthermore, stimuli or events that cause an emotional reaction (music, excitement, and even pleasant smells) can enhance the ability to encode information. (Unfortunately traumatic events are also strongly encoded in this manner.) Exercise has also been shown to increase memory. Indeed, my son learned his math facts through a kinesthetic approach (motor movement) by doing jumping jacks to arrive at the correct answers and retain in memory.

To complicate matters more regarding memory, some people have difficulty in getting the memories encoded as discussed, while others may have difficulty recalling (retrieving the information within their memory). Such problems may have a physical/neurological cause, including stroke or even as seemingly begin as fatigue, while others may be a result of emotional influences. Whatever the differences or limitations, there are researched-based approaches to help better prepare all learners for learning.

Cognitive processes are not only linked to the physical elements but also to emotional interactions, which brings us to the next element of the puzzle: the emotional piece.

Chapter 7

The Emotional Piece

Most beautiful things in the world can't be seen or heard, but must be felt.

—Unknown

Our emotions are central to our overall well-being and day-to-day functioning. Having a so-called bad day usually refers to feeling out of sorts as a result of uncontrollable or unforeseen events within our environment. It is difficult to work as efficiently or even maintain our focus during such times without considerable practice of managing our emotions. Reaching children during their formative years, helping them identify and understand their feelings, teaching compassion, and developing awareness are just as important as eating healthy, exercising, and maintaining cleanliness.

Yet, so often in education we tend to ignore the emotions of children, requiring them to them put aside their feelings in order to better attend to the tasks at hand. This is a task that is difficult for most adults, let alone for a child who may be unable to even identify which emotion is being experienced, let alone how to cope with it.

Nonetheless, we do know that when children are experiencing intense emotions, they would benefit greatly from assistance with understanding and handling this rich and oftentimes rewarding aspect of their personhood. Assistance with the difficult emotions is also critical, including anger, frustration, sadness, and trepidation. Such preparation sets the stage for being ready for learning and ready for life.

Ignoring the emotional lives does not work as we all have seen when frustration and anger gets expressed inappropriately through bullying, acts of revenge, and violence. Sadness and fear might also be unacknowledged and result in depression, anxiety, and other mental health concerns.

A young child who is experiencing temper tantrum needs guidance with understanding and handling the emotions. He or she needs to learn that it is alright to have feelings, but it is how the emotions are expressed that can be helpful or detrimental. All too frequently, children who did not know how to manage emotions were/are labeled as Oppositional Defiant Disorder (ODD), along with other diagnoses, which might then become a self-fulfilling prophecy as parents and teachers begin to treat them differently. Such children believe that they are bad or there is something wrong with them.

Another good example is childhood report cards where children are graded on attitude and behavior (which is heavily influenced by emotions). Thus, a child is graded upon elements that he or she has not been appropriately taught to understand and manage. The result is that children may learn that it can be a bad thing to have feelings.

There have been some attempts over the years to address this disconnect. An Adlerian-based approach called DUSO (Developing an Understanding of Self and Others) was an attempt to introduce this in schools. Unfortunately, it was not widely used and only episodically by guidance counselors who already had unreasonable caseloads!

Furthermore, even this seemingly benign attempt was met by criticism and unfounded fears from extremist groups concerned about, fantasy, mysticism, and even mind control and quasi-religious concerns (Badie, 1993). (Note again the disconnects and paradoxes regarding how this research is used and only sporadically. It seems to go out of favor for the new "fad." Also a disconnect devlops between those setting thee budget and the needs of teachers, students and counselors.

Our emotions are but another way of getting ourselves to pay attention to our needs. By ignoring these red flags, we are actually teaching children, teens, young adults, and indeed all of us that feelings are not important. Nothing could be further from the truth. Feelings can enrich our lives, heal wounds, and even help us rise above our cognitions. This may be the reason there are times when emotions can be so intense, so intricate that they cannot be put into words. Words just cannot do justice to explain all experiences. Understanding and integrating your emotional life is a central puzzle piece to connecting our knowledge about ourselves that our cognitions alone fail to do.

I think most adults can understand that we can know something on an intellectual (cognitive) level, but we really don't fully understand until we have the experience. One of the best examples of this phenomenon is the birth of a child and how profound this experience truly is. Yes, intellectually we know that this event will change our lives, but one cannot grasp the intensity of the emotional experience and how this fills our heart.

Many people use the word "heart," a physical element, to depict where the emotions lie within the body. Of course, in humans the emotions involve a complex process that many people feel physically. Thus, we have phrases such as "my heart is full," or "my heart is broken." Some people may feel the intensity as if their breath has been taken away momentarily or as if they have been "hit in the gut."

Naturally, there may be times when we must put our feelings aside or "push through" our feelings such as fear in order to cope with emergency situations. However, suppressing such feelings may not come without a cost. Sooner or later feelings will need to be addressed and integrated into our schemas of understanding—or the possibility of developing PTSD (posttraumatic stress disorder) or other maladies loams heavily.

Another problem exists however, because parents and teachers have not grown up in an atmosphere where emotions were well valued, and thus our mature population also has difficulty in this arena. The good news is it is never too late and certainly better late than never.

Furthermore, utilizing one element without the others (relying on predominantly on the physical or cognitive aspects of self) is a recipe for failure, or at least for less than peak functioning. As we are learning, humans are complex beings who function tin a synergistic manner throughout their brains and bodies and with their environment.

Congruence is needed to become a fully functioning healthy person. Carl Rogers' theory[1] (one of the most widely researched theories of personality) focuses heavily on the emotional aspect of the individual. It can be understood that a healthy person is someone who:

- Is aware of all experiences and open to both positive and negative feelings (may find even negative ones interesting and intriguing, helping to make sense of these feelings).
- Trusts his or her own feelings (and as a result his or her behaviors are guided through feelings and thoughts).
- Feels a freedom of choice (free will) and is both creative (interaction of physical, cognitive, and behavioral elements) and spontaneous (although not impulsive since the interaction is well processed within the self).
- Integrates and continues to grow and strives to maximize his or her potential.

Dealing with emotions, along with the physical and cognitive development discussed in the previous two chapters, is essential for prime learning. Yet, most schools do little to formally address this aspect of children despite the solid research base, particularly in the neuroscience that demonstrates the important role that affect has in learning. Being ready to learn means being able to identify and work with one's emotions.

Emotions can help us improve our memory of information. Research clearly indicates that cognitive processes are linked to emotional functions. The work of Immordo-Yang and Damasio (2007) refers to the role that emotion has in education as emotional thought. "In particular, the neurobiological evidence suggests that the aspects of cognition that recruit most heavily in schools, namely learning, attention, decision making and social functioning, are both profoundly affected and subsumed within the processes of emotion." (p. 3)

These authors go on to state:

> Connections between decision making, social functioning, and moral reasoning hold new promise for breakthroughs in understanding the role of emotion in decision making, the relationship between learning and emotion, how culture shapes learning and ultimately the development of morality and human ethics. (p. 3)

The implications for educators are immense (but like everything else) will require ongoing research. However for now, we can say that learning and recall of information does not occur in a purely rational (unemotional) domain. And thus, when teachers teach students to minimize the emotional aspects of their studies and function as much as possible in a rational domain, they may be learning the types of knowledge that may not transfer well to real-world situations; just having knowledge is not enough. Students need to be able to apply learning in out-of-school settings where the ability to use such knowledge is heavily nested in the relationships between emotion, cognition, decision-making, and social functioning.

Furthermore, it seems in our culture we too often look at emotions as negative, or something we must tolerate. By ignoring our emotions, we miss opportunities to improve ourselves and our whole culture. For example, humans are able to feel empathy for others. Empathy is the ability to understand the feelings of another without actually having the direct experiences. (Of course, the direct experience can be even more powerful as previously discussed.) With a more direct focus on tuning into these feelings, we may be better able to address problems within our society, such as cruelty, bullying, disrespect, and so forth. Knowledge and reasoning without understanding the emotional and social implications is of little use.

STRESS

As a result of this strong physical-cognitive-emotional link, even the manner in which we experience stress (a factor all of us must learn to cope with) needs serious attention. The need for helping stressed-out students, teachers, and parents is not a new problem. As far back as 1939, Walter Cannon studied the fight or flight response, with numerous studies conducted over the years, indicating that the long-term effects of stress may actually cause permanent damaging physiological changes (McEwen, 2007).

When we combine our understanding of children, adolescents, young adults on to parenthood and teachers, we understand the need for grasping not only the pressures within our society, the day-to-day stressors, but also the physiological changes of the developing individual, which are themselves stressful and the changes occurring psychosocially with each individual as noted by Erikson as far back as 1968.

Julie Lythcott-Haims writing, while dean at Stanford University, reflects that the mental health issues of college students is an increasing worry. Her concerns are founded from a large survey of college counseling centers. Ninety-five percent of college counseling center directors surveyed said the number of students with significant psychological problems is a growing concern in their center or on campus according to Association for University and College Counseling Center Directors survey (Lythcott-Hiam, 2013).

Here again the issue of balance and the realization that our young people are not prepared to handle life's side effects comes into the discussion. It is not that we can totally avoid stress in our lives, nor would this be necessarily preferable. A certain amount of stress may actually be helpful to motivate and get us moving. But too much stress (this will vary depending upon individual's psychology) will make the individual to shut down and not try. Too little stress and one may be unmotivated to even begin as with boredom.

Boredom actually can be looked upon as a specific stressor according to J. Willis (2014) and can have damaging effects to learning and the brain. It also can play into learned helplessness and depression when this form of a stressor becomes chronic. If an individual is constantly experiencing stress and does not know how to cope, he or she may well give up seeing the problem as insurmountable, unrelenting, and impacting his or her whole life.

So, what is the perfect balance? Well, that will depend upon the individual and his or her interaction with the environment. Is it is possible to help students with finding ways to manage stress so that they will not be paralyzed by the fear of failure or even the fear of success—which brings about its own new stressors. In Part Three we will discuss ways that can assist children with coping with stressors enabling optimal learning and preparation for life.

Chapter 8

The Core Piece

> *One looks back with appreciation to the brilliant teachers, but with gratitude to those who touched our human feelings. The curriculum is so much necessary raw material, but warmth is the vital element for the growing plant and for the soul of the child.*
>
> —Carl Jung

Jung was right! The human spirit includes our intellect, emotions, fears, passions, and creativity. There are many names for this core essence, including inner spark, light, life force, soul, or spirit. It is universal in nature and is a basic quality of humanity; it is that aspect of humankind that sets us apart from other living organisms.[1] No matter what we want to call it, this is our true inner self, the pure essence of the person that needs to be allowed to be recognized and understood. It is our inner light and an integral piece of developing readiness for learning and readiness for life.

Core essence need not refer to religious aspects by any means. By being ready on this level, there is an openness to allowing one's inner self (one's spirit) to transcend the day-to-day distractions, to be more focused on what is essential and to be more aware of all of our senses and purpose. It allows for increased creativity, innovative thinking, and even emotional balance.

It is perplexing that in some ways this should be the easiest chapter to write, but it actually is the most difficult—here again another paradox. This core essence of every person is really the embodiment of the One's whole self. Oftentimes, critics may look at this as "crossing the border" with religious beliefs, but that most definitely is not the intent. The core essence is another element of all people, but it probably is something different for all of us as to how we get in touch with our center. Also, it may vary depending upon time and situation, and there are actually many ways to access this dimension of self.

For me it is walking by the ocean, reflective yet reaching for balance and then beyond to what I can achieve. It is the opposite of helplessness. For others, it may be the thrill of rock climbing. Ideally, there will be a special person to help nurture this element in children, so hopefully at some point they are able to provide this for themselves.

Many from the fields of psychology or psychiatry have not dared to delve into this aspect of humans. However others believed that a psychology without understanding this aspect was not complete. It seems Carl Jung was the most interested person in this aspect of humanness. Jung believed: "The human spirit includes our intellect, emotions, fears, passions, and creativity." Emotions must just be experienced on all levels and may even help us get in touch with our true core; understand our true meaning as an individual.[2]

Furthermore, Schermer (2003) describes spirituality as a psychological process (p. 28) the defines our existence and our essence. He does not see it as an "add-on" to our basic drives and energies, but an integral part of them, informing and structuring them. That is, spirituality defines both our existence and our essence, and is not merely a religious doctrine, a pursuit, or a supplement to our basic needs. Deprivation and hunger, for example, may be experienced on both physical and spiritual levels (p. 30).

Every individual has a life force, an inner spark, including atheists, agnostics, or any recognized religion in the world. If we are true to ourselves, this inner life force might become our guide to ethical, moral behavior as well as a compass to lead us toward our unique talents and purpose. This is what I mean here by core readiness.

The pureness of the spirit of a child is the best way to explain this connotation and the risk of losing touch with this aspect of self could be the ultimate cost of living in our stressful society. Ratey and Manning (2014) refer to this as an illness of society. We see it so often and in so many ways in our daily lives and even in the daily lives of our teachers and our children. We can be so caught up in all that needs to get done within a day there is little time left to nurture this side of ourselves.

But certainly, being spiritless is definitely not what we want our children to become. Spiritless means being unengaged, unconcerned, dull, and apathetic—all the characteristics that are plaguing our schools. It is quite necessary to help children understand all aspects of themselves. Research is finally beginning to become more available on this critical need. A quote from Dr. Louise Douce from Ohio State University sums this up well: "For students to learn at their peak capacity, they need to be physically, emotionally, intellectually, and spiritually well" (In Novotney, 2014, p. 37). If students are congruent, or in sync in this manner, they will be much more ready for learning and their behavior will most likely follow to meet their goals.

The inquisitive nature is at the very core of the childhood spirit and is exemplified by children's writers with characters such as Curious George. Unfortunately for the child and all of society, this need for curiosity is crushed under the pressures of our everyday lives and most particularly in our schools with the rigid policies and high-stakes testing practices. Instead, children are required to learn the curriculum in a prescribed manner. For example, they may be diagnosed as disordered if they think differently, or are intrigued (overly curious) about an object or issue.[3] Stifling curiosity also dulls motivation. The focus is not on these critical yet less tangible needs to be fully ready—to be fully present for learning.

We can have children in good shape in terms of cognitive and physical fitness, but ignoring the nonacademics and nonphysical elements relating to the emotions and core spirit is not healthy and counterproductive to optimal learning. It sets up an imbalance or incongruence rendering the individual functioning without utilizing all their ways of absorbing information. Having only our ways of understanding is not a solid foundation for learning fully. This inner core, spark, or life force, is possibly the most essential to learning.

To know one's self on this deepest, most profound level is to be fully harmonious. Thus, knowing one's self on this level requires understanding on all the previous elements, particularly the psychological elements involving cognition, emotions, and ultimately our behavior. However, this understanding of self often does not come without struggle, turmoil, and deep thought. The ideal environment to nurture this process involves a sense calmness and not being hurried. Time to reflect upon the happenings in our lives is a necessary ingredient to nurturing this element.

Dr. David Elkind (1981; 1988; 2001) has written on this topic of the need for time for more than two decades now. Unfortunately today's society is even more hectic than when Dr. Elkind first began to see the need for our children to be able to slow down, not be overly scheduled and allowed to be children.

It is interesting to note that core insights may often come when we have a chance to reflect upon periods of intensity and turmoil in our lives. Yet learning on this level can happen during the most peaceful moments as well, if calmness and time are allowed. So often in our fast-paced society we seem to race from one experience to another without fully processing our lives. Thus, many seem to be without focus or purpose.

Developing a deeper understanding of ourselves helps us form our identities, which can give us a sense of direction and determination to our being. Erikson was correct with the issues involved in forming identity during adolescence, but I do not think his theory went far enough. Identity deals with our core being, and thus we are challenged with identity matters at many times throughout our lives. Such core identity issues may arise when our ethical and moral beliefs are put to the test, and when we make major decisions such as the paths we take throughout our lifetime as partners, parents, and professionals.

Now that people are living much longer healthier lives, research is finding that many will redefine their identities as they prepare for retirement, new careers, and "giving back" to society in a manner that is true to their inner core, in ways that they may previously not had time for because of family responsibilities, finances, and so forth.

If people are able to be aware of their core self, and allow these inner values to be a part of their decision-making process, it may well lead to them making better choices. Individually, it may help some become be less impulsive, be better and more motivated learners, good decision-makers, and critical thinkers, with decreased anxiety and depression: ultimately, a guide to living more fully while being true to oneself. Collectively, with all children being nurtured to develop fully, it could be a catalyst for healthier lifestyles and for a more caring society.

On the other hand, depending upon the teachings in our societies issues of resentment and anger can become toxic. In fact, according to the writings of Dr. Paul Eckman (2008) when interviewing the Dalai Lama, children, in some parts of the world are taught resentment and to hold on to anger based upon actions of others from the past (p. 194–195). Such teachings might overpower the civilized spirit and create an imbalance; these teachings are based on misinformation of one another, misperception. This happens in our society as well, and is at the root of all discrimination, creating a mind-set that does not allow one to move forward and needless animosity and violence within our society.[4]

It should be quite evident by this point the each one of us is much more than the sum of our parts. And with that said, our core essence is still an elusive concept. We are more than just our physical bodies, our brains, and our thoughts; we our ultimately ourselves yet also connected to everyone. It is true that we are all similar in many aspects, but also quite unique and herein lies the possibility for change. The combination of our similarities and differences and accessing our whole selves to work in congruence and collaboration lies the potential to transcend our current conditions for the betterment of self and all beings.

Some of the most critical researchers and clinicians want to be able to measure and quantify and/or break down every part with specialized functions. According to Chopra and Tanzi (2012): "On its own, science, being intellectual, excludes the subjective world of feelings, instincts and intuitions" (p. 171). But people are more complex than the sum of parts, each with a distinct job. It was not too long ago that even the field of medicine did not fully recognize the mind-body connection.

However, we have come a long way with research and more fully understand the benefits and limitations of the differing methodologies. Both qualitative and quantitative methodologies are necessary. Humanness cannot be explained merely through an analysis of parts but also must be understood through our wholeness. Our synergistic interactions are far too complex and idiosyncratic.

No matter how good your methods become, or how sophisticated our technology, there still will be the mystery of our core, our thoughts and feelings, that no machine or test can grasp. We may be able to show the synapses and the chemical electrical processes, but the spiritual aspects remain untapped—our core may transcend our humanness. Thus, to complete this section and transition on to the next chapter, a quote from the National Institute of Health sums up this understanding well. It is clear that even the medical field (with some of the world's best researchers) realizes the "powerful mind-body connection through which emotional, mental, social, spiritual, and behavioral factors can directly affect our health" (NIH, Winter 2008, p. 4).

Chapter 9

The Behavioral Piece

> *When seen as normal and predictable, these periods of regressive behavior are opportunities to understand the child more deeply and to support his or her growth, rather than become locked into a struggle.*
>
> —Brazelton, 1992, p. xviii

The behavioral element is the result or output of the interaction between the physical elements (genetic and biological) and the psychological elements (cognitive, emotional, and spiritual) of the individual (as well as the environment as we shall see in chapter 10) that determines what we do or do not do, in other words our behavior!

In the United States, the physical and cognitive elements are usually best addressed with our children both at home and in our schools. (Of course, problems with neglect and abuse do occur and our schools and medical personnel intervene to assist with these serious infractions.) Unfortunately, it is the psychological elements of the emotional and spiritual aspects that are so often overlooked. Misbehavior is so often the product of this oversight and to which the above quote refers.[1]

However, when there is a synergistic flow among the cognitive, physical, emotional, and spiritual realms of being, we may more easily be ready to learn and thus behave in a more appropriate manner. Even when one of these areas is out of sync, such awareness can help get us back on track to allow for flow or openness to learning more optimally. The child may well be better prepared and on a path toward actualization.

In addition, when the individual has developed specific skills and is able to demonstrate these abilities through his or her behavior, then we can rest assured that this is the most accurate form of assessment there is, showing that one has learned the needed information and can apply it by doing! Clearly you would not want a surgeon who was outstanding on a multiple-choice test, but not capable of using a scalpel skillfully.

Moreover, a solid foundation is being constructed through this type of behavioral output. Once skills are mastered in this manner, they can be built upon to acquire more complex knowledge and abilities to be able to cope with life's difficult challenges and a better way of being.

It is apparent that the behavioral element is closely linked to our physical development and our psychological mind-set. In our schools the behavioral problems are rampant and include not just the obvious acting out through disruptive actions, inattention, boredom, rudeness, bullying, and acts of violence. Of course, some of these children are seriously behaviorally disordered and may indeed need professional interventions from psychiatrists or psychologists. Even the brains of children with severe disorders are different.

Nonetheless, all children misbehave sometimes. This is quite normal and not necessarily a cause for alarm. Indeed, these instances offer wonderful teaching opportunities to assist children and others within the classroom to learn new more appropriate ways of behaving that will not disrupt their learning while still getting their needs met. However, if misbehavior is ignored, children will not learn that their actions are not appropriate and may result in future infractions.

The American Academy of Pediatrics (2015) goes one step further in delineating typical and deviant behavior:

> In reality, the difference between normal and abnormal behavior is not always clear; usually it is a matter of degree or expectation. A fine line often divides normal from abnormal behavior, in part because what is "normal" depends upon the child's level of development, which can vary greatly among children of the same age. (para. 1)

Throughout all of the varying elements discussed thus far, the underlying theme of development must always be keep at the forefront of our work with children. Development occurs within all elements: physical, cognitive, emotional, spiritual, behavioral, and social. In chapter 3, we briefly looked at some of the leading developmental theorists. Social development occurs with interaction between the individual and the environment and possibly with some genetic attributes such as shyness..

Each child develops at his or her own pace. Some develop more quickly with physically related skills such as walking. Oftentimes, we can see gender differences when girls may exhibit fine motor coordination at an early stage, while many boys develop gross motor muscles more quickly. Although caution is in order here since there is a great amount of individual fluctuation between the genders and from one individual to another. The point is that the behavior exhibited varies greatly dependent upon the individual's development in the areas discussed along with his or her interaction with his or her environment.

A child aged two or three years may exhibit temper tantrums; this is a common behavior at this age when the child is exhausted or when he or she does not understand or know how to cope with his or her emotions. The result is a behavioral meltdown or temper tantrum. When my own son was about two years of age, he began this typical, although frustrating, behavior. He would throw back his arms and wail; his head just missing the table or other hard surface. I was concerned that he may accidentally hurt himself. Thus, I explained that it was fine to be angry and frustrated, but he needed to express it in a manner that was more appropriate—in a manner where he would not get hurt!

I proceeded to show him how I would have a temper tantrum and laid belly down on the floor and kicked my feet and flailed my arms in a safe way. Well, he thought this was very funny! Each time after this when he began to meltdown, I would remind him to do it the right way. He would then smile and sit down. This was the beginning of him learning to identify his feelings, understanding that feelings were fine, but expressing them appropriately was important. To this day, he is excellent in understanding his feelings, processing them, and behaving appropriately. (I am not suggesting this approach with every child, but it did work well with him. His language skills were well developed for a two-year-old child.)

What we do not want to see is the inappropriate use of punishment as a way to control behavior. Punishment may decrease certain behavior for the short term, but comes with a heavy list of negative side effects such as anxiety, depression, angry, resentment, and violence. It can crush the spirit of a gentle child and ignite fury in another. Also, children learn to be sneaky and manipulative to not get caught to avoid the punishment. This is counterproductive learning and does not help children learn more appropriate behavior.

On the other hand, well-designed patterns of reinforcement can increase desired behaviors and are more effective in the long run, without the high cost of negative consequences. Of course, with all humans, even young children, it is essential to help them understand the reasons behind the need for certain behaviors, or the absence from others, including the impact it may have on self or others. Here begins the teaching of moral and ethical behavior.

It is also imperative to understand the child's reasoning for certain behaviors, not to excuse misbehavior, but to get to the underlying issues. Unfortunately, typical parental and school interventions do not go beneath the surface to identify the reasons for behavioral issues due to a lack of time and/or training. Left unchecked, such behavioral problems develop into full-blown disorders and comorbid issues of bullying, drug and alcohol abuse, and so forth!

By helping the child identify the issues along with the resulting feelings, and putting the situation into a rational cognitive perspective might heal him or her at all levels, including the core self, and aid in learning new more appropriate ways of behaving, thereby enhancing rather than sabotaging his/her learning and development—not to mention resulting in a more peaceful environment for all.

It is also clear from the research that learning self-control early on reflects in better functioning later. A study by M.E. Dallas, 2015, showed there are potential long-term impacts from behavior learned as a child being linked to better job prospects in later years. Dallas' study showed a solid link between self-esteem and the ability to find employment and maintain a job in later years. Variables of the children's intellectual ability, social status, health, and family issues were taken into account for this study.

Helping children understand themselves, their thoughts and emotions, while learning helpful ways of behaving sets a solid foundation for learning on a day-to-day basis in the classroom and ultimately for handling the world of work and problems of living.

As we proceed on to the next chapter, it should become clearer that the child cannot live in a bubble, and must interact with the environment, a significant and varying influence on the development of readiness for learning.

Chapter 10

The Environmental Piece

> *All children deserve the right to grow up in a healthy environment where they can reach their full potential as citizens of the world.*
>
> —World Health Organization, 2008, p. 2

The age-old debate of theorists and researchers trying to determine if nature (genetics) or nurture (environment) is more important is at the crux of this chapter. Many have wondered over the years if a child was extraordinary because of inherited gifts or as a result of his or her upbringing and education. As you know from the previous chapters, it is not a matter of one or the other, but both—and more!

No individual exists in a vacuum. All of us are affected by our environment, which includes our family, friends, schools, community, culture, and our natural surroundings. The manner in which each person interacts with his or her environment is quite unique due to the complexity of the genetic and psychological differences, along with time and place of interactions.

I have written about these environmental issues before, and there is much that we need to be aware of and much that we can do to make positive changes within the direct environments of the family, friends, schools, as well as the broader environmental influences of our society and political policies. Figure 10.1 illustrates these environmental influences.

Previous publications and research remain spot on, but in this chapter I want to add the dimension of the environmental impacts on the five elements of all individuals: physical, cognitive, emotional, spiritual, and behavioral, with the developmental understanding that children mature at varying rates which is swayed by genetics/biology and the surroundings.[1]

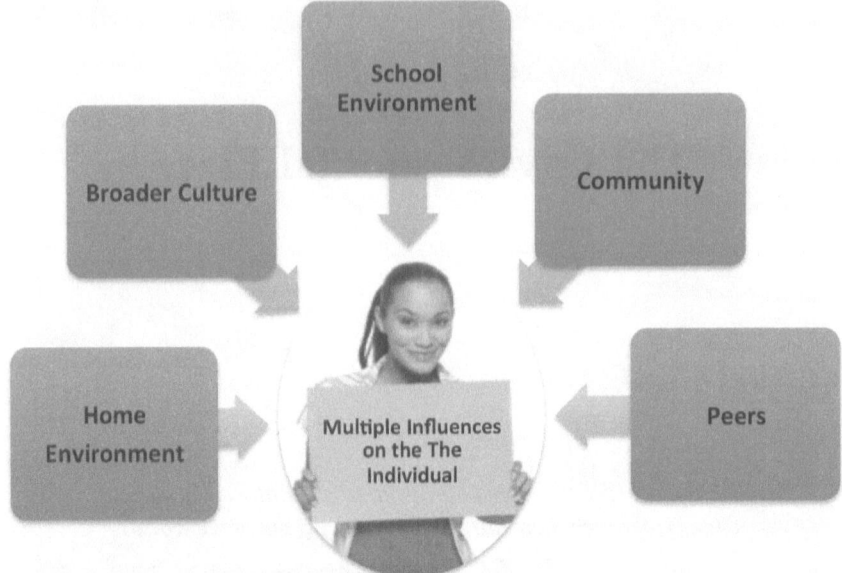

Figure 10.1 Multiple Influences on the Individual.

According to the American Academy of Pediatrics:

> Development can be uneven, too, with a child's social development lagging behind his intellectual growth, or vice versa. In addition, "normal" behavior is in part determined by the context in which it occurs—that is, by the particular situation and time, as well as by the child's own particular family values and expectations, and cultural and social background. (2015, para. 1)

Thus, children can be negatively or positively impacted by outside forces. Herein lies an important key: we already have a tremendous research base of how the environment can be changed to fit the needs of children to learn optimally. It is not that we do not need continued research; this is a given. But we do need to begin to connect and apply consistently (for all children) our current knowledge to our educational and parenting programs.

As with the previous individual elements, the interaction with one's environment and varying settings such as home, school, and community involves a synergy unique to each person. However, as we shall see the environmental factors do impact all individuals either positively or negatively, although unfortunately some more than others.

Let us begin by taking a look at the community/family situations; children residing in less-affluent communities, particularly our inner-city schools, have little access to the schools that have more material, resources, and even more experienced teachers. Many new teachers begin their professional teaching in the inner-city schools, but as soon as possible move to the suburban schools for higher pay and safer surroundings—of course, there are many dedicated inner-city school teachers, and I do not mean to detract from their dedication and determination, but the trend for many capable teachers is to exit these schools as soon as possible.

Many of our inner-city schools are dilapidated with health violations, including mold, asbestos, and lead paint, among potentially several others, which are all clear physical health risks. When children (or school personnel) health is impaired, their readiness to learn also decreases. Previously I have researched parents of children who began school healthy as kindergarteners, and by the end of the year many were on medication for asthma as a result of the environmental mold. It is very difficult to focus when one is constantly sick and the side effects of the medication also may interfere.

In addition, there are the overall community risks in high-crime areas involving gangs, drug and alcohol abuse, and so forth. Even in our most prestigious schools, drugs, alcohol, and bullying exist every day. When children do not feel safe in their schools, little learning is apt to occur. Moreover, safety policies implemented need to be well connected with the research on child development and psychology to understand that some approaches such as staged lockdowns and terror attacks may cause significant emotional harm and scare the children, with the children losing their focus on studies.

This reads well as is true for being prepared for the possibility of threats such as tornadoes or of natural disasters. We certainly want our schools to be built with the necessary safety features and want our children to know how to respond appropriately, but not terrified into thinking that such disasters are common phenomena. On the other hand, underpreparedness for natural occurrences such as storms can be just as threatening when school residing in "Tornado Alley" are not built with storm shelters.

Our country is just recovering from a serious recession, with many families still being out of work. This additional crisis has resulted in many caring parents being unable to provide better situations for their children, including nutritional foods, safe surroundings, and preferred educational opportunities.

Then of course we have the parents who neglect and/or mistreat their own children as a result of their own mental health issues or even lack of education. Such patterns tend to repeat themselves from one generation to the next without appropriate education and intervention. Circumstances are such that children's basic needs are often not met! Learning and coping with life's challenges are focused more on a survival level than on the importance of learning their multiplication tables.

The family stressors are also at an all-time high. Furthermore, few parents have education or training with managing their own lives, let alone being able to help provide the necessary foundation for learning and life for their children! Unfortunately parenthood does not come with a "how-to" manual.

Young adults have been thrown out into "the real world" upon graduation from high school or higher education with little, if any, real-world preparation! If they are fortunate they may have parents or mentors who have been able to successfully navigate the many transitional and situational obstacles presented over a lifetime. Most are not so fortunate since so many adults are struggling in our communities; all one needs to do is watch the local and national news and see the reflection from the increase in the number of prescriptions for anxiety, depression, and other mental health concerns.

The concern of being overly hurried in our fast-paced society affects all of us on many levels. For example, physically there is little time to eat healthy and it seems we are a society addicted to fast foods. Likewise there is little time or energy left for adequate sleep and exercise.

The social development of our children has changed dramatically as well. Children are overly scheduled from one activity to another during the afterschool hours, creating another form of stress and disjointedness to the social maturity. Rarely can children play freely anywhere. Schools have to meet such stringent curriculum goals that recess and free time is cut from the day.

Many parents are concerned with the safety of their children playing in the local neighborhoods or parks and are constantly supervised. It is unfortunate that we must worry so much about the safety of our children—although we do! As a result, children learn our world is unsafe, which increases their anxiety, but they do not learn how to cope with these cognitive and emotional aspects. They never really learn how to rely on their own skills and abilities which crushes their confidence.

Dr. Peter Gray (2013) has researched and written extensively on this need for children to have free play. He sees these changes away from free play as a great loss to our society.

According to Gray:

> The drive to play freely is a basic, biological drive. Lack of free play may not kill the physical body, as would lack of food, air, or water, but it kills the spirit and stunts mental growth. Free play is the means by which children learn to make friends, overcome their fears, solve their own problems, and generally take control of their own lives. (p. 5)

Gray's argument is solid and appealing: children are by nature equipped to learn, on their own initiative, and possess knowledge and skills necessary to survive within their culture. By allowing children to be themselves and play freely, they are ready for learning and ready for life.

However, the argument on the other side of the coin might be that our world has changed so drastically from the more uncomplicated times of early tribes people, but at the very least we have found our current state of attempting to get children ready for learning and ready for life so far out of balance that this basic need of all children (and it would not hurt adults either) to play more has been suppressed to the point of being almost nonexistent.

We have forced all children, young adults, and even our elderly into very stifling environments within our schools, many forms of brainless employment, and in the elder years into nursing homes. Such sterile environments set up a "prison like existence," one that can only be endured by disengagement. Then to make matters even worse we diagnosis and categorize our people, disrespecting their uniqueness and focusing on their weaknesses.

Such approaches are obviously doomed to failure, but nonetheless the process continues. We do what we have been taught before, and add insult to injury by including more of the same that has caused the problems in the first place: longer school days, more homework, more high-stakes testing, less time for recess, less exercise, less time for sleep, less time for eating, more junk food, less time for social activities, and less time (if any) to integrate our thoughts, feelings, and behaviors.[2]

So the question remains: How can we better prepare all learners from the very young, to those approaching young adulthood and higher education, to those of the baby boomers? On to the next chapter to bring these disconnects!

Chapter 11

The Synergistic Process

The good life is a process, not a state of being. It is a direction not a destination.

—Carl Rogers

Putting together what we have learned thus far in part II, we can now better define what I mean by readiness for learning and readiness for life. Such inclination involves a process of development in the individual elements discussed: physical, cognitive, emotional, spiritual, and behavioral, along with the interaction with one's environment as illustrated in figure 11.1. It should be well understood that although there are many developmental guidelines that can assist with understanding the needs of children, it is equally, if not more, important to consider the uniqueness of each individual in the psychological elements that are so often overlooked.

If all goes well with this synergy, the individual should be more inclined toward learning and mastering knowledge and skills. Of course, no individual has the perfect combination of factors or experiences that set the foundation of ideal readiness. Nonetheless, there are many research-based options to ensure that the foundation and learning process is as optimal as possible.

Some will encourage the development of learning through a person's strengths, while still helping to foster the other capacities. At times, the environment may need modifications that can enhance the well-being of all students. With such adjustments, readiness can be augmented for students to be ready, willing, and engaged in learning; the gaps in learning will be bridged; integration can be achieved.

Figure 11.1 depicts the individual's interaction with his/her environment. With specific interventions and environmental adjustment, the individual is ready, willing, and involved in learning. The key is working together

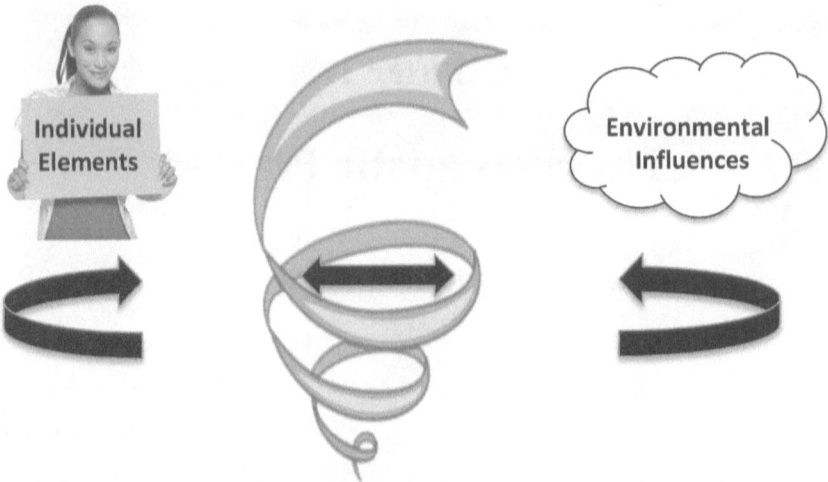

Figure 11.1 Individual and Environment Factors.

in an integrated manner. That's what synergy is all about: parts working together within the individual and individuals working together within their environment.

BASIC PRINCIPLES FOR DEVELOPING READINESS FOR LEARNING AND READINESS FOR LIFE

This whole ready-for-learning, ready-for-life approach is a process that needs to *begin as early in childhood as possible*, yet we should not be pessimistic about starting where we are at in life; is never too late. Also, it is not just the responsibility of the child, the parents, the teachers, or administrators; it requires an integrative process where all are involved to create and maintain a healthy climate in which one can learn, grow, and be ready for life's challenges.

Most of the focus in this book is on preparing young children for learning, but the fact of the matter is that most people, at all ages, are poorly prepared to deal with life's challenges because of a disruption in their earlier faulty, incomplete, or surface learning. (Although I am also very interested in this process as we age, my focus in this book looks primarily at children and those preparing for college and young adulthood.)

Having worked in colleges and university settings for more than twenty-five years, it is clear to me that many young people are not prepared to be away from home for the first time or manage the responsibilities required both academically and socially. Many universities are recognizing this problem and are focusing on developing "coming of age" programs for these young adults, recognizing the stress affecting this age group.

In addition, according to Ben Locke from Penn State, there are very clear and concerning trends that indicate that college student mental health is declining, not improving. The statistics on the use of medication with incoming students supports this theory. Thus, this 18 to 25-year-old cohort is very often unprepared for higher education and managing the responsibilities of young adulthood.

Developmental Considerations

So let us begin with the research that emphases the importance of considering total development of the individual. Our brains are much more malleable than realized previously, yet we also need to take into account that learning may be more difficult and resistant at certain times in one's development. Thus, Stamm (2007) specified the need to teach children at the appropriate times developmentally and teach information correctly the first time!

If you remember back to an early theory of Lev Vygotsky, his concept of windows of opportunity appears to hold true! At certain times in human development, some subjects are easier to learn (i.e., foreign languages earlier).

Thus, although children's brains are more plastic than previously realized, the importance of adequate preparation cannot be stressed enough. When children are well prepared on all levels for learning, the process may be both more efficient and effective.

The reader should keep in mind that some approaches may be right for some people and not others. The intent here is to present approaches and techniques, which have been shown by research to assist people. Although most people may find these methods very helpful, there always should be periodic review and follow-up to determine effectiveness, allowing for further modifications if needed. Furthermore, although these areas have been broken down into physically and internally based interventions, it should be clear that there is an integrative aspect at work; physical interventions such as exercise, yoga, and play stimulate all aspects of the individual.

Okay, so we know that no child comes with a perfectly balanced, ideal set of attributes that allow for optimal learning. Thus, research-based interventions need to happen that will help minimize the areas of weakness and maximize the strengths of each child. Certainly regular medical care, good parenting, and so forth are necessary, as we have discussed, but the interventions presented here are in addition to the basics that all children need to flourish.

It is important not to forget that more traditional forms of learning are also important and all previous approaches out the window! However, what we most definitely do need are supplementation approaches and alternatives that lay the foundation for optimal learning that is deep and can be applied by the learners. Furthermore, this is not an exhaustive attempt to present all the outstanding evidenced-based approaches that help children learn. The intent is to present several approaches and studies that seem to best illustrate the points and have been very influential in preparing children to be ready to learn more optimally. It is my examination of these interventions which may well be advantageous to preparing children for optimal learning by stimulating elements that may have been under utilized or not integrated previously.

As you read through the next several chapters, you should notice that there is tremendous overlap with the positive benefits of these research-based interventions to all aspects of the entire individual: brain/mind and body become activated and integrated. Attention to the whole individual, one's uniqueness, and developmental levels and quirks should be at the forefront of our thinking when applying and of the practices. Also, any methods used should be well aligned with individual, parental and, when indicated, medical consent.

We shall see that these interventions impact the whole child cognitively, emotionally, behaviorally, spiritually, and physically; thus, they can help each/all aspects of the individual. Furthermore, evidenced-based research has been able to show the outward expressions of the individual's behavior and even in some cases, the changes within the brain and the body documenting the astonishing mind-body interaction.

Any one approach alone is not enough. It will take a consistent, integrative collection of approaches, which will vary according to the individual and at varying times within the development of the individual. By understanding the individual's strengths within the elements physically, cognitively, emotionally, behaviorally, spiritually, or their areas of weakness (untapped or suppressed elements), interventions can be tailor-made.

This may seem overwhelming at first, but with approaches that address each element, children will learn to access these different dimensions of self, allowing for growth in these areas. Furthermore, children (or adults for that matter) can be taught to assess their own balance and adjust accordingly. (This is the ultimate preparedness for managing life's challenges!)

Let's summarize the basics of this interactive process all requiring an underlying premise of *time and freedom*, of not being overly scheduled, rushed, or pressured. Then the individual and environmental needs can be minimized or enhanced (depending upon need) to assist each individual with developing optimal readiness.

Physically: Provide a healthy lifestyle through regular medical checkups, nourishing food, adequate sleep, exercise, as well as safe and healthy environments.

Cognitively: Develop an optimistic outlook. Take time to think things through for mastery and reflection for deeper learning.

Emotionally: Take time to identify, understand, and process emotions.

Spiritually: Be true to yourself.

Behaviorally: Choose behaviors that align with your true self and are congruent with your thoughts, feelings, and physical abilities. Behaviors also should acknowledge and respect *others and the environment* in which you interact.

Environmentally: Working together collaboratively to establish a healthy, optimistic climate for all to flourish. A collaborative and cooperative team approach consisting of parents, educators, students, political policymakers, healthcare professionals, and interdisciplinary researchers are all necessary to develop and benefit the environment. This is how we can make a difference and get the changes we need. This is how we can be ready for learning and ultimately be ready for life.

Part III

THE INTERVENTIONS AND DISCUSSIONS: RESEARCH-BASED INTERVENTIONS TO PROMOTE READINESS FOR LEARNING AND FOR LIFE—THE PARADOXES CAN BE RESOLVED AND GAPS CAN BE BRIDGED!

Don't become a mere recorder of facts, but try to penetrate the mystery of their origin

—Ivan Pavlov (1849–1936)

Our young people are at serious risk academically and psychologically. The tremendous stress that youth are under is due to developmental changes along with the pressure from society, government policies, teachers, parents, and peers, all trying to compete in our global arena. It can be overwhelming to the whole person: physically, cognitively, emotionally, behaviorally, and even with one's core. It is up to us to provide them with a better way of being, based upon solid research, that will allow them to grow, learn, and flourish.

In the subsequent chapters interventions that are not the typical approaches currently used in most of our schools will be discussed. However, they are based upon solid research and some with decades of practice. Integrating these within our parenting approaches and within our schools will help bridge the disconnects and paradoxes, while helping each individual learn to access all elements of their being, physically and psychologically to allow for optimal readiness and deeper learning.

Chapter 12

Getting Ready Physically

Predominantly Physically Based Interventions

> *In my experience, no development line in a child proceeds in a continuously upward course. Motor development, cognitive development, and emotional development all seem to proceed in a jagged line, with peaks, valleys and plateaus.*
>
> —Brazelton, 1992, p. xix

With the above quote in mind, in this chapter, we will consider the predominantly physically based interventions as in each area there is an interaction of the mind and body at work. Although these approaches may involve exercise or movement, the whole person reaps the benefits, and it does not need to involve a sweatshop mentality. It can and should be fun as to which reinforces the likelihood of sustaining the practice.

Regular movement is a necessity of living. Children would never learn to walk if they had not been motivated to move their legs and build up the muscles to be strong enough to hold their bodies; behavior of standing, balancing, and taking a step took courage and practice to master this skill. (One can see that even though we consider walking to be a physical ability, being ready to learn to walk involves much more, both physically and psychologically.)

Furthermore, the additional benefits from being active and making exercise a regular activity a part of everyone's daily routine include decreased obesity (a serious problem with our youth). And over the lifespan (which we are trying to get our children prepared to handle), regular exercises reduces the risk of many serious illnesses and improves mood and mental well-being, as well as one's chances for a longer, healthier, active and safer life. (Hyde, Maher, Elavsky, 2013) Thus, exercise along with nutritious foods must become the rule to support the healthy development of the children for optimal functioning. Healthy, nutritious, balanced meals are also essential.

Knowing the research is very clear on the need for regular movement, it seems perplexing to look at rules in our schools that require children to sit still not allowing for this inherent need. Some children are better adapted to be able to sit still than others, but may well be counterproductive to their learning as well. (It seems that rules are often developed as a matter of convenience and control, rather than research-based needs of people).

Other forms of exercise also have proven results with children in schools, but have yet to be applied and a comprehensive manner. Dr. John Ratey's and Eric Hagerman research (2008) indicates there is a positive connection between exercise and brain performance; exercise improves one's ability to learn, counters high stress levels, helps reduce and even prevent maladaptive anxiety, reduces depression, while increasing levels of focus and attention.

Their program involved fun exercises that were technologically programmed in Naperville, Illinois. Not only did it help with fitness, but it was instrumental in elevating the local school district of 19,000 kids to a world-class level in science test scores (Ratey & Hagerman, 2008).

Rewarding forms of exercise set a pattern of behavior that helps keeps us healthy and prepared throughout a lifetime. With all of the influences and safeguards that movement provides, the benefits continue throughout the life cycle, including hormonal issues for women, coping with addiction, and even helping to aging wisely. It sets up the foundation to help us prepare for an optimal life.

Even dance, a behavioral expressive form of movement/exercise, is demonstrating remarkable results of using it effectively. Koch, Kunz, Lykou, and Cruz (2014) conducted a meta-analysis of the dance therapy effect indicating that both dance and dance therapy movement have positive outcomes, including improvement in quality of life, reducing depression and anxiety, maintaining body image, and overall well-being, all important for people to be ready for learning.

Dance movement therapy has shown, through research outcomes using clinical trials, to provide numerous benefits for many populations of varying ages. It helps to improve mood, self-concept/self-esteem, and body image. Studies also suggested an improvement with social relationships, academic performance, stress management, self-regulation (behavior), and capacity for empathy. For more information, consult the American Dance Therapy Association (ADTA), which follows the highest licensing and standards. This approach uses techniques that are appropriate for all populations, benefitting even those with limited physical abilities.

More recently:

> DMT has begun to contribute many evidence-based studies on its effects (e.g., Bradt, Goodill, & Dileo, 2011; Karkou & Meekums, 2014), and can be rightfully

called one of the foremost contributors to evidence based clinical literature on the effectiveness of body-mind interventions." (Cruz & Koch, 2015, p. 11)

Dance, as a fun and rewarding form of exercise, may be quite beneficial as well, without the added dimension of therapy.

Exercise was also shown to be strongly correlated with increases in brain mass and cell production as well as improved cognitive processing and regulation of mood (In Sousa, 2010, p. 15). Exercise (movement) should be a regular part of everyone's daily routine and does not need to be viewed as work or have proficiencies developed to determine how many sit ups a ten-year old should be able to do! It can be achieved through free time, recess, and play.

Play is one of the best ways for children to get exercise as well as to learn and help prepare them for being ready to manage life's tasks. I found it fascinating and affirming to read the work of Dr. Peter Gray (2013) from Boston College, who writes:

> In the name of education, we have increasingly deprived children of the time and freedom they need to educate themselves through their own means. And in the name of safety, we have deprived children of the freedom they need to develop the understanding, courage, and confidence required to face life's dangers and challenges with equanimity. (p. 19)

I could not agree more and a further perplexing issue is that play does not need any formal rules; indeed, it should not have such restrictions or it is no longer play!

According to Gray (2013):

> Education ... is cultural transmission. It is the set of processes by which each new generation of human beings, in any social group, acquires and builds upon the skill, knowledge, lore, and values—that is the culture—of previous generations within that groups. (p. 24)

How better to accomplish this goal than through play. Play also allows for modeling adult behavior, including equality, sharing, cooperation, and collaboration. It is a great preparation for learning and life.

As with any adult role we value in our society, it becomes clear that it takes more than knowledge to be competent. It takes experience. Play helps with this as children role-play and model adult behaviors as parents, and even with various careers. Such role-playing allows the imagination to help integrate these experiences into appropriate repertoire of skills and behaviors.

I have been teaching at the college/university level for more than twenty-five years now. It is evident that many entering freshman are often poorly prepared to manage their lives even in terms of scheduling and time management. Frequently they have not been prepared, taught, or allowed to take responsibility for their learning or their lives. Teachers forced to micromanage their students to demonstrate learning and helicopter parents may well contribute to this observation.

Furthermore, children have been overly scheduled with one adult run activity after another, their expectation is for someone to tell them what to do next. Even as young adults, aside from playing with their iPhones there often is little self-initiated direction.

Allowing children to be responsible at a relatively early age is essential for their learning. No one can force a child to learn any more than you can force a horse to drink. Teachers can only do so much, but through early engagement and early acceptance that each child is repsonsible can help immensely.

Even when a child demonstrates inappropriate role-playing through his or her play; this can yield insight to the adults that additional educational and/or psychological interventions are needed. Case in point, the child who exhibits abusive behavior with his or her dolls or other toys might, in fact, be trying to express a cry for help in the only way many young children are able to, through play.

Some naysayers may believe that this is time wasted. Nothing could be further from the truth. Finland schools have the shortest school day and a significant amount of outdoor play time, yet are at the highest-performing levels on the international Programs for International Student Assessment (PISA). exams. (OECD, 2012)

In addition, countless studies, over many decades, have successfully utilized such "play therapy" interventions to address the mental health needs of children. Play can help prevent future mental health issues from developing and can offer a safe outlet for the expression of emotions, which may be overwhelming and thus disrupting the child's readiness for learning and overall development.

Along the same lines, there has been a significant increase in the development of mental health issues in our society. A psychology professor and researcher from San Diego State University, Dr. Jean Twenge has conducted extensive analyses of changes in young people's scores over time on two measures: MMPI and Taylor's Manifest Anxiety Scale. Both scales have been used with young people for decades. The results are very concerning and reportedly almost 85% +/− of today's elementary, high school, and college students have scores greater than those of 50 years ago, with between 5 and 8 times as many of these young people scoring at levels which suggest anxiety or depressive disorders. (In Gray, 2013, p. 15)

Likewise, more and more college students are beginning their challenges away from home ill prepared to deal with this more independent role academically, as well as socially and emotionally. More and more teens and young adults are prescribed antianxiety and antidepressant drugs than ever before. Some may believe that clinicians are more adept at diagnosing disorders, but the statistics do not necessarily reflect this viewpoint.

Yoga also offers the potential for physical benefit as well as a balance between mind and body (according to Khalsa & Gould, 2012). They clearly remind us that yoga is not a religion, but a contemplative mind-body practice. It does not require any beliefs because it is biological (p. 77). They continue explaining a connection as well with preventive medicine and treatment for a variety of maladies. Khalsa and Gould explain specific and detailed research on the benefits of yoga on the body and on the brain, including improvements in concentration processing and motor speed, and in computational skills as well as help rewire the brains of those with attentional-related disorders.

Yoga also has the potential to improve feelings of peace and well-being. Khalsa and Gould see yoga as a potential tool for all students worldwide to improve academic performance. Indeed, Khalsa and Gould assert that yoga can change your brain structure along with the biochemistry! The traditional approaches such as Hatha Yoga are better known in the United States. Such an approach involves physical postures and exercises and might include deep relaxation techniques, breathing techniques, meditation, mindfulness, as well as understanding the psychology and philosophy of yoga (pp. 78–79).

Yoga

According to Sat Bir Khalsa, assistant professor of medicine at Harvard Medical School and a neuroscientist at Brighman and Women's Hospital in Boston, Massachusetts, yoga means "to yoke" or "union." The goal of yoga is to unify and balance the mind and the body (p. 11). He explains that "tradition yoga involves not only the physical postures but also breadth control, deep muscle relaxation, meditation, and mindfulness practices" (p. 11).

He also explains that yoga is not simply a hobby or a sport, nor is it a religion, nor can its benefits be dismissed as a placebo (p. 4). It is also more widely practiced than many may realize; reports suggest that one in ten people now practice yoga in the United States (Khalsa and Gould, 2012, p. 4). In India even airline pilots and crew members practice yoga in order to cope with their job stress (Weingus, 2015)!

Yoga offers benefits in multiple areas of the mind-body connection, including physical, emotional, and spiritual. Like meditation and mindfulness techniques, yoga can help students obtain a readiness that includes a sense of calmness and peacefulness to help cope with stress, elevate one's mood, and increase mental sharpness (p. 9).

Furthermore, there is compelling neuroscientific support that yoga can actually change the brain both chemically and structurally. fMRI studies suggest show positive changes occur in the brain regions responsible for attention, body awareness, high-level cognitive functioning and self-perception (Khalsa and Gould, 2012, pp. 11–12).

In addition, yoga can help build resilience to stress, which is useful throughout one's life time at difficult periods of life transition. It can assist with getting deeper more restorative sleep, increased benefits physically, and improved attitudes and perceptions Khalsa & Gould, 2012. Dr. Khalsa's work has been extended to evaluate the effectiveness of yoga in school settings with children and adolescents for both mental and physical health and prevention (p. 4).

Robin Lowry (2011), from Temple University, conducted a survey of youth yoga curriculum. The findings show that yoga is being recommened for fun, physical education and even as a health strategy. Furthermore, assisted with selfawareness, focus and relaxation.

The results indicated there was little consistency or integration into the curriculum or assessment strategies to determine yoga's helpfulness. However, this is not necessarily a problem; it should specify where more work is needed. Such programs are relatively new in our schools, but do need to be developed and implemented professionally. Here again teachers will need additional training.

The differences with these approaches here is that children are not forced to do sit-ups or run a mile under a specific time limit. Such forced approaches certainly are quite measureable, but set up conditions of competition and more stress, at which only a few athletically endowed children may excel. Those less inclined often give up (believe themselves incapable, become emotionally anxious or depressed when forced to participate, their sense of self is deflated, their spirit crushed, and healthy behavior is not reinforced). Avoidant behavior, including sneaking and lying to get out of gym class, become the name of the counterproductive approach.

Even when children have true neurological differences, such as those with ADHD, physical activity can help release pent up energy or in some cases stimulate the child to be more focused and ready. Indeed, there are many children diagnosed with ADD who actually may be tapping their pencil or wiggling in their chairs as means to keep themselves awake and focused! So, without any doubt our schools should be increasing (not decreasing) regular physical and fun exercise every day and even several times a day.

Time, freedom to move, and space are the needed *environmental modifications*. Of course, adequate nutrition enhances this aspect as well. Children should be allowed to have access to healthy beverages and food when they are hungry. This also can assist children to focus on their internal needs and to rely on these cues, to know when to eat and when they have had enough. Fuel for the body and for the brain is essential to overall learning.

Thus, Dr. Ned Hallowell (2011) sums up well about preparation of the physical body and brain for learning:

> To think well, the brain requires oxygen, glucose, and a host of nutrients and other factors, all of which get depleted over time. Without the right diet, sleep, exercise, and physical supports (good lighting, air supply, chair and desk, and so forth), the brain will underperform. (p. 33)

Chapter 13

Getting Ready Cognitively
Mainly Cognitive Interventions

> *The principle goal of education in the schools should be creating men and women who are capable of doing new things, not simply repeating what other generations have done.*
>
> —Jean Piaget

How true this quote from Jean Piaget still rings. *The manner in which one thinks impacts his or her* readiness for learning ready for life. One's mindset can impede learning and thus this brings us to a needed discussion on optimism and resiliency. Martin Seligman's well-researched approach to teaching "Learned Optimism" has not been used across our schools despite excellent results in numerous studies.

Back in 1990, Seligman wrote about his research in *Learned Optimism: How to Change Your Mind and Your Life*; in 1996, he focused more on the children and schools in the *Optimistic Child*, and more recently in 2011, he looked at ways for all of us to reach for a better way of being in "Flourish."

In the *Optimistic Child*, he equates "Learned Optimism" to being inoculated against life's challenges, by developing a positive outlook toward life, and an internal explanatory style over one's ability to make changes within our situations. This involves the perception of control one sees in situations.

For example, with a healthy optimistic outlook, a child may see his or her difficulty with learning to read as a challenge, but one that is obtainable. A child with true dyslexia may also explain this challenge, not as a global problem with himself or herself, but a small facet of one's makeup that can be managed when teachers teach him in a way that he learns best.

Yet, here is another example when diagnosis can sometimes be quite harmful. If the child interprets the diagnosis as a problem with his or her full being and starts to explain it as he or she is not capable because he or she can't learn as quickly as the other children, then this perception can spread into all areas of the person affecting emotions, increasing possibility of depression, anxiety, frustration, acting out behavior, and/or giving up—just as Seligman's dogs did in his original studies leading to the concept of learned helplessness.

Taking away anyone's sense of control over their lives increases a pessimistic mindset and is strongly related to depression whether one is an infant or a centurion. Believing one has some control over situations helps pessimism breed hopelessness and affects our well-being greatly.

A good example of this issue is discussed by J. Willis (2014). She explains that boredom is a specific form of stress and can damage the brain.

In most classrooms today, teachers are confronted with an excess of curriculum and standards that must be met. However, there are vast differences among students, some who have mastered the material, while others who do not have an adequate foundation of knowledge for mastery. Either way students turn off developing a negative mind-set and the stress of boredom is the result. (Form a learning perspective we know that skills should be achievable, but challenging for each individual. Too difficult and they may give up, while too easy and they turn off.)

On the other hand, optimism breeds hopefulness and can increase motivation and stamina to keep trying and a positive sense of well-being. The good news is that we definitely can teach optimism by addressing these pessimistic thoughts which strongly influence emotions (creating anxiety and depression), decreases one's sense of self (core); and ultimately impact behavior. But here we need to address the major disconnect with the research and practice. We know how to create more optimistic outlooks, but our practices and policies do not go along with the findings.

Stress and Resiliency

In addition, we know that optimism breeds resiliency. Resiliency is a quality that allows one to bounce back from setbacks more easily. Furthermore, according to Elizabeth Hoge, MD, meditation can also help improve resiliency offering an important tool for developing the quality of resiliency, helping to deal with stress. As a result it is critical to help parents with parenting skills and their own stressors in order to provide healthy relationships that can either prevent or help heal early relationship wounds.

The CDC reminds us that when we learn to cope with stress, our resiliency is enhanced and we actually grow (psychologically) helping to manage the stress. Furthermore, resiliency has the added benefit of increasing motivation.

The ACE Study Adverse Childhood Experiences is one of the largest investigations ever conducted to assess associations between childhood maltreatment and later-life health and well-being. The analysis is a collaborative effort between the CDC and Prevention and the Kaiser Permanente's Health Appraisal Clinic in San Diego (CDC, 2014).

It is critical to understand how some of the worst health and social problems in our nation can arise as a consequence of adverse childhood experiences, including those that are most central to students' level of achievement and overall success in later years.

On the other hand, too much stress establishes a propensity for illness, and dysfunction of the process involved with memory also negatively impacting learning and coping with life's transitions. Thus, we also need to help teachers understand the connections between stress, resiliency, and attachments to help their students as well as themselves. Teachers are at particularly high risk of suffering burnout due to the sheer weight of the responsibility they carry every day caring for the lives of numerous young people and charged with making sure they learn as well! Learning to prepare and safeguard themselves helps everyone in the long run.

Chapter 14

Getting Ready Emotionally
Largely Emotional-Based Interventions

If you are anxious, you can't learn. It's like dropping seeds on concrete. With a quiet mind, people take things in

—Dr. Herbert Benson

Emotionally Based Interventions: Identifying and understanding children's emotions is a critical component to help them cope with life and behave according to life's norms. Being able to cope with emotions also helps to prevent one from becoming overwhelmed with anxiety, depression, and other forms of emotional distress.

Dr. Hallowell expresses needs beyond the physical ones mentioned above. He states: "Other ingredients matter too, such as a feeling of hope, personal control, optimism, and gratitude. These emotional factors all contribute to optimal brain/mind function" (p. 33).

Judy Willis, who is both a board-certified neurologist and a classroom teacher, knows how important emotions are with learning. She also recognizes the research/practice disconnect as well. Willis explains that the research from the 1990s tends to support the earlier theories of James, Vygotsky Piaget, Kashen, Dewy, and Gardner among others; however, the neuroscience implications for learning and the brain are to date only suggestive of how the brain learns. (In Sousa, 2010, p. 46).

Thus, in other words, both the previous theories discussed in earlier chapters along with the more a specific neurological research offers some understanding, but not the entire story. She asserts that teaching strategies that have been developed from well-controlled neuroimaging research are at best compatible with the research to date about how the brain seems to deal with emotions, environmental influences, and sensory input (In Sousa 2010, p. 46).

This should clearly illustrate the dire need for teachers to become trained about the brain as well as understand and conduct research to be able to better develop appropriate teaching strategies, curriculum, and individual student interventions. Additional training in understanding and conducting research will help them fine-tune the interventions and be able to determine when such approaches are working.

"For students to learn at their peak capacity, they need to be physically, emotionally, intellectually, and spiritually well" (Louise Douce, Ph.D. OSU in Monitor September 2014 article by Novotney).

SPECIFIC INTERVENTIONS THAT HELP INTEGRATE EMOTIONS: MEDITATION AND MINDFULNESS

Meditation basically is contemplation, taking time to quietly reflect upon something. Some people meditate on certain thoughts or it might be a sound, an object, a visualization, or a sensation. It can be done while sitting quietly or even walking. Mediation can help us feel calmer and come to a better understanding through meditations. It can result in deeper learning.

> Western science, for the most part, has devoted itself to studying nature and what's observable in the outer world. Basically, meditation is about bringing the same kind of systematic discipline to understanding inner phenomena, and that, too, is a legitimate field of investigation for science. You could call it the science of subjectivity, of first-person experience, of interiority. (Jon Kabat-Zinn)

Furthermore, according to Chopra and Tanzi (2012): meditation can help access one's core or as they call it "real self, and even improve one's genetic output. "That is, the right genes get switched on and the wrong ones switch off" (p. 72). The potential here is really quite amazing, implying it is conceivable that we are not as determined by our nature or nurture.

(Dr. Deepak Chopra, MD, is well known for his work in the field of alternative medicine. He is also a fellow of the American College of Physicians and a member of the American Association of Clinical Endocrinologists and a physician trained both in internal medicine and in endocrinology. Dr. Rudi Tanzi is the Joseph P. and Rose F. Kennedy Professor of Neurology at Harvard University.)

Mindfulness is closely related to meditation according to Chopra and Tanzi, as they describe the best way to cultivate mindfulness is through meditation (p. 254). They go on to assert that mindfulness "is self-monitoring without casting blame or judgment (p. 256). Thus one may become more aware of thoughts, feelings, tastes, and overall experience in the present moment. It has the potential to decrease maladaptive functioning such as impulsive behavior.

On the other hand, mindfulness can increase appreciation and sensation of the pleasant taste of a raisin, for example. Oftentimes, we may call someone who is unaware as mindless. People who are not mindful are self-centered to connect with other people; they lack sensitivity in many social situations (p. 252).

Herbert Benson and Jon Kabat-Zinn are two of the best-known pioneers in the field of mind-body medicine. Benson is affiliated with Harvard Medical School and Kabat-Zinn with the University of Massachusetts Medical School. Both of these renowned institutions have used meditation, mindfulness, and yoga practices in order to help people with a wide variety of medically related problems, including chronic illness and chronic pain.

According to a APA report on stress in America, teenage stress is at an all-time high. The town of Newton, Massachusetts, an affluent suburb of Boston, has a contract with the Benson Henry Institute of Mind-Body Medicine, at MGH, to help distress the high teenage stress rate. Teachers and staff members were trained with stress reducing technique, including yoga, meditation, and breathing exercise that are now used in the classroom (Zimmerman, 2014).

Dr. Benson is well known for his research and writing of the book "The Relaxation Response," can decrease stress through training. The RR can be stimulated in many ways, including yoga, deep breathing, tai chi, and imagery, to name a few. According to Wilcher: "What we have found in our research is that kids [who learn these self-calming techniques] improve their grades, their work habits, school attendance, lifestyle and behavior, they feel less stress and more in control, their self-esteem goes up, they become more inner directed and less influenced by peers" (Zimmerman, 2014, para. 16).

Furthermore, in 2012 Foret, Scult and Wilcher, Chudnofsky, Malloy, and Hasheminejad and Park reported working with the Needham Public High School to help students learn manage stress through a relaxation response-based curriculum designed to promote stress management and increase resiliency and overall well-being. Researchers also wanted to determine if it was feasible to complete the intervention. Although the results were promising, there were issues that needed to be addressed including follow through with online home assignments.

The Mind Body Medical Institute (MBMI) at MGH in Boston has provided training for students and teachers through its Education Initiative (EI) since 1989. Marylin Wilcher, senior director from the Benson Henry Institute, has worked with more than 100 schools in the United States and Canada. Clearly, efforts are being made to integrate neuroscience research into our schools, but the efforts are too few and far between.

In addition, other sources such as licensed psychologist and related practitioners could impart training to people. Yet, because of the high cost of individual services for mind-body training programs, most people do not have access to these services except through program trials or research studies. Health insurance may cover some of the costs if the individual is diagnosed with a significant illness requiring such services.

Using mindfulness-based techniques may also help bridge cognitions to emotions and allow for the deeper self-understanding within one's very core. This is one approach that has been used in many cultures for thousands of years. It need not be confused with religious practices; it involves being more in tune with one's self.

Remember from chapter 1, psychiatrist Daniel J. Siegel (2007) expressed his concern over the current state of the problems within our culture and our schools. He stated:

> We are in desperate need of a new way of being—in ourselves, in our schools, and in our society. Our modern cultures has evolved at times to create a troubled world with individuals suffering from alienation, schools failing to inspire and to connect with students, in short, a society without a moral compass to help clarify how we can move forward in our global community. (p. xv)
>
> Mindfulness can help us be ready for life challenges because [it] can help us embrace, rather than resist, the inevitable ups and downs of life equip us to handle human predicaments. (Siegel, 2010, p. 25)

Siegel (2007) asserts that mindfulness, an age-old practice with new cutting-edge research, is an approach with demonstrated evidence of the physical, psychological, and social benefits that can help. Learning mindful approaches—learning to be more attuned to all that is happening within and around ourselves—allows us to be fully involved in the experience of learning, to understand others better and to understand self. Furthermore, being mindful may help with behavior, so that actions are not impulsive, but experienced cognitively and emotionally and are congruent with our true self. It even can foster empathy and acceptance helping to make our schools "bully proof" and safer (Siegel, 2007).

The Kabat-Zinn duo (1997) have even developed a mindful guide for parents to help themselves become fully present and consciously aware of the "engagement in parenting." Having awareness, known as mindfulness, leads to deeper insight into and understanding of our children and ourselves. The Kabat-Zinns suggest how mindful parenting can be healing and transformative for both children and adults (In Journal of Child and Family Studies, Vol. 12, No. 2, June 2003 (°C 2003), pp. 247–249).

Such applied mindful programs are already being used in some schools. However, this may be an example of a reverse disconnect where enough support and training for the educators is not available, although the results appear helpful. Thus, it is important to make sure there is no disconnect not only between research and practice but also between applying the research accurately, which so often happens in the field of education. Research, support, and training for the educators are essential.

Mindful approaches have been used successfully to help level the playing field with children from low-income families, as well as to help cope with stresses and trauma. It also assists with learning to calm one's emotions, focus, and how to cope, as opposed to being reprimanded for, with disruptive behavior without knowing how to make the needed adjustments. Mindfulness can help the child acquire the needed self-skills.

One such approach was developed by J.G Larochette, founder and director of the Mindful Life Project.

According to Larochette:

Before we can teach a kid how to academically excel in school, we need to teach him how to have stillness, pay attention, stay on task, regulate, make good choices. We tell kids be quiet, calm yourself down, be still. We tell them all these things they need in the classroom, but we're not teaching them how to do that. (In Swartz, 2014, p. 2)

Larochette's approach targets the issue of students not being ready or prepared to learn. He states: "When we look at low performing schools it's not that these children are unable to learn, it's that very often they are unavailable to learn" (In Swartz, 2014, p. 2). The benefit of using mindfulness and meditation appears to help the student as well as the overall environment in the classroom. Larochette specifically mentions these ways of nurturing congruence within the individual "improves self-control, helps children to cope with trauma, improves overall school climate and students learn to help one another cooperatively." Critics may be concerned with how improvements could be measured and indeed Larochette was able to determine that incidents of referrals and detention, suspensions declined (In Swartz, 2014).

Chopra and Tanzi, Siegel, Eckman, and even the Dalai Lama support the use of meditation and mindfulness in our schools.

OTHER INTERVENTIONS THAT TAP INTO THE EMOTIONAL REALM

Even animal-assisted learning can be extremely beneficial for many, whatever the age level. Animals have been used to help reduce the physiological reaction to stress (In Geist, 2011). Furthermore, numerous studies have demonstrated the effectiveness of animals assisting with such psychological issues as ADHD, PTSD, conduct disorders (In Geist, 2011). The use of animals as assistants in therapy of learning is not as new as many may think. Sigmund Freud often had his own dog present at sessions! However, Boris Levinson, a child psychologist who worked with children experiencing muteness or were detached, is considered the founder of animal-assisted therapy. He viewed his dog being present at sessions as a transitional object for the client. Improvements in the client were readily observed.

Although to this day there remains a critical need for more research in this area, there have been some well-documented research, including studies by Allen (1991); Friedman (2000); Kogan (1999); and Katcher and Williams (1994). Although there is difficulty to assess the unusual abilities that animals seem to exhibit, almost a sense that is beyond our human abilities, to tune into the needs and problems of humans that is uncanny; such interactions have been well documented over the years where dolphins help humans in distress; horses that have helped autistic children overcome many of their issues, mute children beginning to speak, and the list goes on and on.

Animals as readiness assistance are well worth a try, under good supervision. Animal assistance can be used as a supplement to other interventions and particularly when other approaches have not succeeded.

Furthermore, specific fields of study such as art and music help children become ready for learning. Mary Helen Immordino-Yang EdD and Antonio Damasio (2007) have done considerable work with connecting the brain, emotions, and cognition to education. When considering the role of affect in education they talk of emotional thought or: "The aspects of cognition that we recruit heavily in schools including learning attention, memory and decision making and social functioning are profoundly affected by and subsumed within the process of emotion" (p. 3).

They also clarify that:

> connections between decision making, social functioning, and moral reasoning hold new promise for breakthroughs in understanding the role of emotion in decision making, the relationship between learning and emotion, how culture shapes learning and ultimately the development of morality and human ethics.
>
> Some may use the more neutral term "metacognitive thinking," which basically is being aware of and monitoring one's thinking. Hardiman (2001) suggest very easily integrated techniques to help students develop these skills. She presents using reflective discussions of lessons to foster the habit of reflection on learning and the use of reflection journals (p. 55).

The implications for educators are immense (but like everything else) will require ongoing research. However, for now, we can say that learning and recalling of information does not occur in a purely rational (unemotional) domain. Therefore, when teachers train students to minimize the emotional aspects of their studies and function as much as possible in a rational domain, they may be learning knowledge that may not transfer well to the real-world situation.

One of the misconstrued ideas that is currently plaguing education involves the belief that the arts are less essential than the science, technology, engineering and mathematics: STEM subjects. Creativity and assistance with developing competency in the STEM subject areas are enhanced by a strong foundation in the arts. Furthermore, arts are key to accessing parts of the brain dealing with emotion and helping acquire deeper learning as well as be in touch with our whole selves.

According to Immordino-Yang and Damasio (2007) "emotional thought" which is highly correlated to learning, attention and memory, decision-making, and social functioning is also strongly influenced by emotion and thus should have direct bearing on how we work with children to assist with learning. Furthermore, benefits of musical training include improved verbal memory and reading ability in children as well as in adults (Gaab, Tallal, Kim, Lakshminarayanan, Archie, Glover & Gabrieli, 2005).

Furthermore, there is a connection between emotion and creativity, a cherished asset which may be dulled if the emotion is not sensed. Blunting creativity hits at the very core of the childhood spirit and has negative ramifications for thinking outside the box and developing different ways of problem-solving.

Thus just having knowledge is not enough; students need to be able to apply learning in other settings which requires an understanding of the emotional and social aspects in order to make appropriate decisions. The knowledge without the complete understanding is of very little value.

Chapter 15

Getting Ready with Our Center
Chiefly Core Interventions

We must make the choices that enable us to fulfill the deepest capacities of our real selves.

—Thomas Merton

CORE ESSENCE: OUR CENTER

This brings us to the next element which in reality is not separate from the others, but functions as a whole. Being in touch with who we are, what is right for self, as well as our sense of moral thought and behavior are strong aspects of our core sense of self, our core, or our spirituality. By being core ready, I mean an openness to allowing one's inner self (one's core) to transcend the day-to-day disruptions, to be more focused on what is essential, to be more aware, allowing for increased creativity. It is all that makes us unique as well as all that makes us one with humanity and nature. Our core is our compass toward actualization.

Schermer and Kingsley (2003) talk of spirituality as "a capacity and motivation for living fully ... the 'psychospiritual self,'" and it is a "self which is connected both to everyday realities and biosocial necessities" and also develops throughout the lifespan (In Counselman, 2005, pp. 323–326).

Whatever one wants to call it, core, center, psyche, spirit, or essence; no matter if one is an atheist, agnostic, or shares in a religious ideology, there is the realization that there is something that is higher than ourselves. Life, our very nature is not fully understandable, explainable in totally human terms. Thus, people marvel at the birth of a newborn as miraculous. The mystery of the coming together of sperm and egg can be explained in medical terms—to a point, but there is something more. It is this "more" that is discussed here, the unique center of each being.

Humanistic theory and educational approaches capture the importance of the self, emphasize developing a sense of responsibility, identifying the meaning of one's existence, and the uniqueness of each person (Burger, 2008, pp. 288–289). Moral development and behavior is also linked to this element.

We may remember from an earlier chapter that the humanistic movement where Abraham Maslow and Carl Rogers were presented as trailblazers to this approach. Seeing all people as equal, looking for the good in humans, and demanding equality and the respect for the rights of all beings are the hallmarks of this approach that can help prepare each child to feel safe, valued, and respected, laying down the initial foundation to readiness.

Humanistic interventions can also have a more optimistic outlook, promoting resiliency allowing one to learn to cope with stress. Diagnosis is not essential for this viewpoint since the individual is viewed in his or her entirety, a unique and valued individual with varying strengths and weakness, as we all have. Interventions are developed as ways to enhance the sense of self.

Here is where parents and educators must be careful. A healthy self-concept is based upon realistic feedback, not false praise. When children are praised for efforts that are made halfheartedly or not earned, self-concept and thus self-esteem are actually harmed. Psychologist Stanley Coopersmith back in 1967 conducted a solid research study, but the results were misconstrued and misapplied. (Here is another example of a disconnect between practice and research.)

Chopra and Tanzi (2012) also believe that humanistic traits are essential to internationally engaged education for excellence and flow well with this first universal value of humanity. A humanistic approach also blends well with both Eastern and Western traditions that "view compassion as a universal condition, shared by the human mind as a whole" (p. 285).

There are many ways to access this core within our selves. Schermer identifies meditation and prayer as one way. (Although prayer may not be the approach of choice for some people, but it is right for many. On the other hand, meditation is thinking as described above and may be preferred by others.)

Yoga, discussed above, unites several practices, including the physical positions, with meditation and mindfulness. When yoga is practiced over time, it actually can change one's brain and help an individual function better as a human being physically, mentally, and emotionally, with the possible added benefit of taking him or her to higher levels of spiritual fulfillment (Khalsa & Gould, 2012, p. 77).

Developing the important sense of responsibility can be obtained. Referring back to developing a healthy core, more responsibility must be placed on the shoulders of the students. Overly controlled school environments can rob students of their need to develop the understanding that education must be earned, and that ultimately they are responsible for obtaining an excellent education. It is not something that can be given; it must be nurtured and developed over time (Gunzelmann, 2014).

Practicums, internships, and service-learning interventions can all help with developing a healthy sense of self, assist with identifying one's purpose (meaning) in life. At the same time these experiential interventions make learning come alive while giving back to the community, fostering healthy cooperative and collaborative relationships.

On the other hand, there are some practices that can erode the very core of individuals. Any form of discrimination or learned animosity may corrupt the very center of any young child. Disrespect for diversity and a lack of open-mindedness occurs in many settings and many cultures. In some parts of the world, children are actually taught to be bitter and conserve the anger of their ancestors according to psychologist Dr. Paul Eckman (2008, p. 194) in conversation with the Dalai Lama.

Such a negative mind-set can erode the very core of individuals and society, preventing optimal learning and not allowing us to move forward. This is not to say that previous tribulations will be forgotten, but we do need to move forward, forgive and find ways to live together cooperatively and collaboratively for the good of all. Since the core is often associated with moral thought and behavior, the importance of an awareness of this element and understanding its function as a compass or guide to direct our lives cannot be emphasized enough.

It may seem puzzling mentioning *technology* within this chapter on one's spirit. Yet, some look toward the future for technology to take care of all of life's problems and certainly holds a very strong place in education. There is no doubt that technological advances can assist with helping children rewire their brains to overcome a variety of issues, and even specifically when applied to learning to read (Shaywitz, 2003; Simos et al., 2002).

Yet we do need to keep in mind that technology is merely a tool and one that can be implemented to improve learning. But a caution is in order here:

No matter how good technology becomes there still will be a uniqueness of our thoughts and feelings that no machine can understand. It can show the chemical and electrical activity at the synapses, but it is the spiritual intuitive visceral aspects that still remain untapped. Students, teachers, and parents may find their purpose for being through their center.

Animals as Helpers:

Last, but certainly not least, animal-assisted learning and animal-assisted therapy can be the missing link for many requiring with learning glitches, including emotional, cognitive, physical, or behavioral problems. According to Lori Friesen (2010):

> Animal-assisted therapy and activity are useful modalities that can be easily incorporated into the counseling and school setting. Animals in counseling sessions and the classroom facilitate an atmosphere of trust, nurturance, and relationship building. Animals actually help a person to focus on a task because of an interest in interacting with the pet. The therapy animal is a non-judgemental companion in the process of learning and development. (p. 261)

Animal Assisted Learning holds an important place in helping children, youth, adults, and even the elderly. Boris Levinson has been credited with being the father of animal-assisted therapy (1969). Levinson's dog would often be in his office during therapy session where he noticed improvements in his clients. However, since the early years, it has been used in a variety of settings, although the research is limited.

However, there have been studies assessing the benefits of animals with adults, adolescents, and children (Friesen, 2010, p. 261). In addition, animals have been in many classrooms and are becoming more popular.

> Research over the past 30 years indicates that therapy dogs may offer physiological, emotional, social, and physical support for children both in therapeutic in a school setting. The underlying general assumptions according to Friesen are: "children appear to perceive the dogs as non-judgemental participants who are not involved with the expectations or complications of human relationships." (Friesen, 2010, p. 261)

Animal-assisted approaches are becoming increasingly more common and appear to have significant positive impacts, lasting for more than one setting. Friedman in 2000 found that using a dog helped to moderate the stress responses better in children than the presence of an adult. Kogen et al. (1999) found students with an emotional disorders in a school setting were able to make progress toward their IEP goals gaining emotional control, fewer tantrums, and so on. Furthermore, according to Ascione and Weber (1999), animals can be helpful in school settings to help reduce violence while improving overall humane attitudes toward animals, which also generalized empathy toward people (In Friesen, 2010).

It seems as if animals offer physiological, emotional, and social support for children who appear to view them as nonjudgmental participants. The animals are emotionally supportive and company for the children, without the overbearing feeling that they are being analyzed, tested, or otherwise graded. This provides another layer of safety for taking risks for the shy or anxious child.

Animal-assisted literacy programs have happened in both school and library settings with the children reading to the animals. Reports from parents and educators suggest children become more confident and enthusiastic about reading (In Friesen & Delisle, 2012). They can be a tremendous source of support for many in schools, offices, or home settings and should be strongly considered as a supportive adjunct to other approaches.

Furthermore, children with autism spectrum can benefit for animal assistance disorders, severe behavioral issues, and a variety of other issues, including attentional disorders, learning disabilities, emotional disorders, and even physical disabilities may benefit from animal-assisted programs. The bonds that can develop between an animal and a human is different than a human-human bond, but can be very intense, powerful, and healing. They can foster an appreciation for life, for humans as well as all for creatures, in a manner that helps individuals transcend life's iniquities. Animals may help us all learn to care for one another and coexist in ways that are experiential—a better form of learning.

There is no doubt that more research is needed in this subfield using animals, but this clearly works for many people where other approaches have not. Animals can help overcome resistance, increase motivation and even reach to the very core of people.

The love of all living creatures is the most noble attribute of man.

—Charles Darwin

Chapter 16

Getting Ready Behaviorally
Generally Behavioral Interventions

How you react to every experience modifies your neural network and, thus, the world you live in.

—Chopra and Tanzi (2012)

BEHAVIORAL INTERVENTIONS

When there is a synergistic flow among the cognitive, physical, emotional, and spiritual realms of being, we may more easily be ready to learn and live more optimally on a path toward excellence and a better way of being.

Behavioral problems are rampant in our schools and communities and add stress and disruption to many. Dealing with behavioral problems has stimulated considerable research over the years. Some of it has been applied often in schools and at home, but there are many misunderstandings creating a disconnect from the research to the application. For example, many people misunderstand the powerful concepts developed by B.F. Skinner. He looked at any behavior (healthy or maladaptive) as response from reinforcements within the environment. A behavior will increase if reinforced either positively or negatively.

Many mistakenly equate negative reinforcement with punishment, and this is a serious problem because of the many harmful side effects of punishment. Unlike negative reinforcement, punishment decreases behavior. But children may learn other things along with decreasing the punished behavior. He or she may learn to be fearful, anxious, may become depressed, or may learn to be more sneaky so as not to get caught, or build up anger and resentment which can result in acting out behaviors.

In our schools interventions such as missing recess and suspension are all punishments and thus in danger of the above side effects. In addition, they are usually not effective with repeat offenders as many may actually be trying to get out of the classroom, thus actually reinforcing unwanted behaviors. Missing recess and class time is also detrimental to the goal of establishing a healthy foundation for learning readiness. Punishment is not the way to go under most circumstances—case in point, just look at the recidivism rates in our prisons. Reinforcement works better without the above side effects.

Schedules of reinforcement must also be considered. For example, with a very young child, just beginning to learn a new skill, it may be appropriate to reinforce the desired behavior on each occurrence, yet it is unreasonable and unhealthy to expect this to continue in a classroom setting of 20 or more students and also does not help the child learn to reinforce himself or herself for learning. With various schedules, behaviors can be reinforced and allow for self-reinforcement, leading the students to be intrinsically motivated.

Differing schedules are better under differing situations, and thus the reader may want to become more attuned with these reinforcement schedules, which we all are motivated by. For example, for adults, money can be a reinforcer. If one knows he or she is going to be paid depending upon how many apples picked in a day, this may increase apple-picking behavior; however, the quality and ripeness of the apples picked might be affected. Each schedule has benefits and drawbacks. Ideally, we want to establish learning as the reinforcing stimulus for the child (or adult, for that matter).

More specifically, yet based upon the above learning theories, there has been significant research aimed at helping reduce aggression and behavior problems in children. Some of the best have come about from the work of psychologist Ross Green (2010). His underlying philosophy is positive, believing that kids will do well if they can. He believes that children who experience severe behavioral problems are delayed in their development of crucial cognitive skills issues, with adaptability, problem-solving, and ability to tolerate frustration. (Keep in mind that this is the crux of being ready for learning and ready for life, to help the development in all areas.)

Thus, he looks at these issues from a three-point perspective. First, understanding the child and what area(s) are delayed is critical. Second, identifying the specific situations when behavior occurs; third, solving the problem and teaching the needed skills (Greene, 2010). His work has utilized research from the fields of developmental psychopathology, prevention and neuroscience, along with excellent clinical observations with persuasive results.

Back in 1996, researchers at Boston College designed a program for inner-city middle-school students who experienced problems with intense emotional arousal that often lead to behavioral problems. Dacey, DeSalvatore, and Robinson (1996) taught two relaxation techniques aimed to develop skills and attitudes of self-control. Although it appears the intervention was well accepted and helpful, as usual there has been little follow-up and more compressive application of these techniques.

Civic engagement and/or service learning: Where children become socially involved in a caring and responsible manner with others. This not only adds depth to learning and reinforcement to learning. As neurologist R. Tanzi and Dr. D. Chopra assert: "The issue is the rewards you receive through bonding and connection, the basic process that makes a peaceful social engagement is important as is intellectual/stimulation for health of brain and helps to make a more peaceful society" (p. 301).

Psychiatrist E. Hallowell (2011) also expresses the benefit students can obtain from becoming involved with others. He believes that connection is a very important factor to prevent problems from developing. If a child feels connection at home and connection at school, he or she is not likely to get into trouble.

SELF-CONTROL AND CONFLICT RESOLUTION

Darcey, DeSalvatore, and Robinson (1996) taught middle-school students skills and attitudes of self-control in an attempt to address conflict prevention; they were specific interventions for those with conflict issues.. Although this study appeared to be successful it does not seem to be implemented in any meaningful way since then.

Ideally these interventions go along with the interventions used in all elements of the person, that is, mind and body, to not only fix behaviors that are counterproductive, but also promote readiness for learning and throughout life. The skills learned are not just band-aid fixes to put the lid on a behavioral outburst. Indeed, these can intervene in a restorative manner.

Chapter 17

Getting Ready Environmentally

Essentially Environmental Interventions

> *It is the whole educational environment that can either be conducive to learning or detrimental, toxic or healthy.*
>
> —Gunzelmann, 2014, p. 122

The quote above requires an addition, for it is not only the school environment, but the culture, the communities, and the home that impact one's readiness. Consideration and nurturing of the environment in which children learn and grow is no small influence on preparing for learning and life. A relatively new field of research, *social cognitive neuroscience*, involves both the social aspects with the cognitive understanding of the brain attempts to explain the impact that the environmental influences of culture and climate have on learning. "School culture is characterized in part by open communication, level of expectations, amount of recognition and appreciation for effort, involvement in decision making, and degree of caring" (Sousa, 2010, p. 16).

Almost anything can negatively impact the environment creating a climate that is not conducive to thriving. Having written about these issues extensively, before it may be helpful to review a few of the key concepts here which can impact all children, and keep in mind that it is not just these influences within the schools!

TIME AND SCHEDULING

First and foremost a discussion on the issue of scheduling is in order.

Early start days are not in the child's best interest for learning. Depending upon the age of a child, adequate time for *rest and nourishment* should be the priority. Teenage students sleep/wake cycles differ developmentally, not just because they want to stay up later. Their *circadian rhythm* actually changes with the changes that occur during puberty according to Hagenauer, Perryman, Lee, and Carskadon (2009).

Furthermore, disruptions in the cycle can actually harm the organism and disrupt the health and well-being of a person. In turn the approximately 45% *sleep deprived* teens (NSF, 2000) will not be well set for learning. Following the child's natural circadian rhythm can also help to promote learning, being ready to learn.

Likewise increasing the *length of the school day* is not in the child's best interest either, particularly if the same old approaches continue to be used. Such changes come at the expense of other requirements for play, exercise, fresh air, socialization, family time, and so on. Furthermore, increasing the length of the day will increase stress levels and may even increase student disengagement and dropout rates.

The school days in Finland, an educational leader, has much shorter school days, beginning around 8:00 a.m. and finishing around 12:00–2:00 p.m. depending upon the group, not to mention they have hot healthy and free meal served family style with time to interact with peers and teachers! Well run after school care to Safe and balanced after school care is provided allowing children time to socialize and play, while parents are able to devote their energies on their work until around 4:00 p.m. when parents and children have time to spend together (Virtual Finland)!

Time issues are also problematic even within the regularly scheduled school day which is jam packed with one class right after another, 20 minutes for lunch, including time waiting in line. Children may be deep in the learning process, when they are disrupted and forced to change to the next subject. This makes little sense in terms of all that we know about the learning process. It cannot be forced or rushed and certainly should not be disrupted.

Time is needed for reflection, to think about what one is learning, to fully integrate it, make sense of it and allow it to get into one's long-term memory. Our current "hurry up and rush" to the next class, with little time between disrupt this process greatly.

It is also inaccurate to say that all children have short attention spans. It is more accurate to say that *the attention spans* of child differ. Many young children are content and focused for extended periods of time with movies, games, projects, reading, listening, or viewing if the material interesting and developmentally appropriate. Some children may need extended time, not because they have a problem, but because their learning can go deeper as a result. (Special accommodations, such as extended time are currently used only with a documented disability. Accommodations should be available to all children without the need for a label.)

Even the concept of diagnosis in schools is destructive. Parents, teachers, and even the child himself or herself might misconstrue their disability, to see as different, as damaged goods; the spirit is wounded and depression or other dual diagnosis often result. (I do see disabilities as only looking at the negative, when there are always positive aspects; for example, many learning-disabled children are the most creative and innovated thinkers.)

Psychoeducational diagnoses are not the same has having strep throat, where the physician can give you a prescription for an antibiotic and it goes away. Once diagnosed, these psychological disorders stay with the person and end up being engrained in the self-concept. An alternative healthy and helpful approach can be taught.

Remembering back to when my son was 8 or 9 years old and attending a private school based upon a multiple intelligences philosophy, he commented upon another little boy who seemed to be experiencing some difficulty. His response could not have been better. He explained that the other boy did have difficulty with certain things, but he's really good at other things, just like everyone.

In addition, there appeared to be no cases of bullying happening in this school. Older children would stop and help a younger child when needed and there was an atmosphere of trust and respect—not out of fear, but out of reciprocity. They treated others modeled after what they had seen, heard, and experienced. The climate within the school, reflected in the *attitudes* and *behaviors* of the educators, exuded a *healthy optimism* and *respect* for one another.

Just as current policies tend to overschedule the school day, resulting in disjointed/disrupted learning, the same seems to happen all too often in the after-school hours when concerned parents over schedule their child's free time. Dr. David Elkin was one of the first to write about the phenomenon in *The Hurried Child*.

The "hurried child" syndrome has only gotten worse; now we are seeing the "frazzled child" as a result. Down time, play, socialization, and family time are all essential to de-stress and find support, acceptance, and solace without needing to continually perform. Everyone needs time to just "be," which brings us to the all-important issue of *toxic testing*, which not only adds to the frazzled child problem but can also contribute to a highly dysfunctional environment.

Across the country, we have a continued movement toward accountability, increased use of standardized tests, and high-stakes testing. Along with these trends come the negative symptoms of teaching to the test, test anxiety, lowered self-esteem, misunderstandings of children, and missed opportunities for many. Administrators are under pressure to demonstrate student learning and are therefore teaching concepts at earlier ages. Doing so results not in greater knowledge but in added pressure for our children to measure up and to hurry up their learning (Gunzelmann, 2008; 2012; 2012).

Traditional assessment methods are fostered by the big business of the testing and are continued in use due to the convenience and ability to compare scores across groups of students. Yet these tests are expensive and might not represent the ability of students to critically analyze information and creatively solve problems. Notwithstanding many students test poorly on certain formats of tests, even when they know the material well! In fact, some of our brightest and most capable students do poorly on multiple-choice tests, thus not showcasing their real competencies.

Furthermore, such testing may set up an unhealthy competition among students and educators, which might result in side effects of cheating and teaching to the test. This is a misuse of testing, but unfortunately happens quite often.

Outdated testing approaches focus negatively to show what a child does not know or what is wrong or deficient with his or her abilities rather than what is valued and unique about the child's particular way of learning, coping, reasoning, and problem-solving. It is important to understand what is missing in a child's repertoire in order to remedy this area of weakness, but it can be done in a better way.

What really is important with learning is that one develops knowledge and problem-solving skills that can be applied. After all, I would much rather have a surgeon who was able to demonstrate his or her abilities rather than one who scored at the top of the class on a multiple-choice exam! *Competency-based approaches* allow for this form of determination and can be used in a helpful, affirming manner.

Competency-based education has other values as well. Not only is it the answer to cut costs as in college tuition (students can finish earlier) if they demonstrate their competency, but it addresses issues of motivation, corrects for boredom, and shows real learning. Students take responsibility for their learning, which becomes in engaged process, and is no longer a passive process of spoon feeding.

It is a form of authentic assessment where students can actually do rather than through often misleading results of many types of standardized assessment.

Grade inflation becomes a thing of the past—either the student can meet the competencies or they need further work and the areas of focus are identified.

Furthermore, such methods can cut teachers' time down and allows them to assume their real role as guide rather than being the impossible source of all knowledge attempting to funnel piles of facts into the students' memory. It can even give teachers time to work with those students who need it most!

Government Support

Being ready for learning and ready for life needs to start earlier than the formal education years. Stamm (2007), a neuropsychological expert, clearly emphasized that learning begins so much earlier. However, this does not imply that children should not begin attending formal schooling earlier, but that *parents must be provided adequate time and parenting skills* to be with their children in helpful ways. Also, in our fast-paced society, many parents do not have adequate time or resources to provide such conditions. Parenting programs, well-run daycare and preschool programs are a necessity.

Schools and home settings need to be healthy and free from *environmental toxins* too. The hidden dangers within our school buildings and homes negatively impact children's readiness for learning and may even effect the long-term health and well-being of everyone. Problems such as radon, asbestos, lead paint, molds, poor air quality, pesticides, and cleaners all need to be taken into account and remedied.

Having written about these issues extensively before, I found it extremely alarming how prevalent these problems are in our schools and communities. This is an area that needs government officials to step up and clean our living and learning environments. It goes without saying that all of our schools should be safe and healthy.

It also is a priority of our president to make opportunities *equally available* to all and must fund the development of well researched based *early intervention programs that are safe, healthy and sustainable* for all children. In addition, although progress has been made toward assuring health care for all, we still have a long way to go to assure that all children have access to healthy food and healthy home environments. Too many hard working, devoted parents are unable to give their children these basic essential requirements. If we are really committed to making learning opportunities equally available to all, we need to make sure that the foundations to optimal learning is provided.

Part IV

BRINGING IT ALL TOGETHER AND HOPE FOR THE FUTURE

Our young people are at serious risk, both academically and psychologically. The tremendous stress that youth are under is in part due to a myriad of factors. There is no reliable way to predict every stressful situation an individual must confront: there are some that we all have in common (such as learning), but how these situations affect each person is highly variable. It can be overwhelming to the whole person—physically, cognitively, emotionally, behaviorally, and even with one's core. It is up to us to provide them with a better way of being, of being prepared, and able to cope and excel, based upon solid research, that will allow them to grow, learn, and flourish.

Chapter 18

Ready for Learning and Ready for Life in a Nutshell

At the core of who we are is the roots of those that have influenced our lives the most and the impact of what they have exposed us to is always there and when the foundation is laid with love and commitment, our lives at some point will reflect that of which we have been taught.

—Aja Graydon

I CAN DO IT!

The above quote comes from singer and song writer Aja Graydon, who expresses well the concepts behind being ready for learning and ready for life.

Becoming ready, striving toward optimal learning, involves making the best of our genetic inheritances and other influences. Even when some aspects may be out of our control, there are always ways to intervene on one level or another to strengthen and improve ones' ability to function while increasing psychological and physical well-being.

Balance   Understand   Integrate   Practice   Push On

Figure 18.1   Being Ready.

- Balance our life appropriately: sleep, food, exercise, play, and so forth.
- Experience involves being fully engrossed in living and learning.
- Integrating understanding of one's experiences on all levels of personality: cognitively, emotionally, spiritually, and behaviorally.
- Practice new wisdom and techniques to ensure these advances become a part of your repertoire of functioning. (This is not done through workbook pages and other thoughtless approaches, but through useful ways of using learned material.)
- Push on: It is a natural need for humans to move toward further development. Thus, motivation is a natural occurrence to push on toward mastering more knowledge, skills, and use information in innovative ways (if one's creative nature (spirit) has not been squelched).

GROWTH SPIRAL

Once we have acquired the process of accessing elements of ourselves, which previously may not have been a part of our learning, we are more prepared for growth and learning, indeed ready for life. We can handle stress and even use it optimally. We all start out in life with a lot to learn. Establishing a healthy lifestyle that stimulates growth in all areas. This is based upon understanding, integration, practice, and balance that help us be stronger, more resilient, and better able to cope with difficult environmental concerns, thereby making good choices for ourselves and others to deal with all of life's challenges. Thus, one's growth spiral may start out small at the bottom, but our learning grows exponentially.

It involves a growth spiral and a synergistic working together, both individually and collectively. It will help each individual master needed

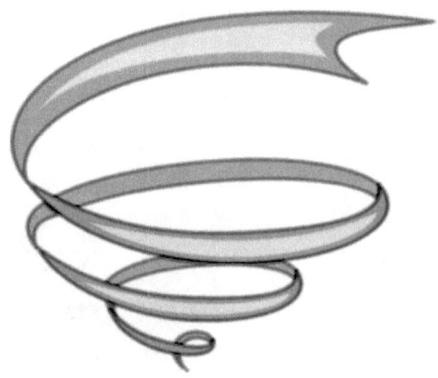

Figure 18.2   Readiness Growth Spiral.

skills and provide interactive collaboration to handle the developmental transitions at all stages of life, thereby hoping to solve many of the world's problems.

Chapter 19

So Where Do We Go From Here???

And in order to succeed in later life, you need creative skills because look at how fast the world is changing.

—Robert Sternberg

That of course is the ultimate challenge, the fast-paced changes that we all are confronted with on a daily basis! So, where do we go from here? Well, I suggest we reach beyond readiness.

1. Research needs to be *ongoing* and *interdisciplinary*, with *qualitative* and *quantitative* studies to get the whole picture of the person's readiness needs. There will be a need for refinement of approaches, to tailor techniques for every individual, along with advancement in technology and other tools to guide improvements.
2. Appreciate the need for individual work, but also the need for to come together in a cooperative manner. Some people do their best work while on their own, but we also can combine the information adhered by individuals.
3. *Cooperation, collaboration* and *commitment* among the researchers, policymakers, educators, parents and students, working together to meet the needs of all children.
4. Implementing the research-based approaches in a comprehensive manner. Training needs to be provide for our educators and parents to work as effectively as possible. It should not be implemented on a hit-or-miss basis.

5. Teaching for humanity and with compassion. It does require understanding and desire to live together and for benefit from one another (humans and earth's creatures and taking strides to prevent further climate decline).
6. Support, encouragement, and backing of the healthy policies within our schools and communities and ensuring that newer research approaches receive this same respect and support.
7. Allowing teachers to be the professionals they can be, not tying their hands through counterproductive policies and testing which interferes with learning and satisfaction.
8. Development of safety policies that do not terrify students needlessly, which are not so dependent upon cost—just get the equipment in place.
9. The fixing of environmental issues that impact development negatively, along with the implementation of safety policies that enhance learning and well-being.
10. Healthy development needs to be equally and available to everyone.
11. Helping people at all developmental stages and ages: those going off to college and coming of age in our complex world, those attempting to manage graduate school, coping with meeting the financial costs of living, along with the needs of their growing families, the middle years climbing the social, career/economic ladders; becoming a husband/wife/parent, coping with issues of their aging parents, and transitioning to retirement. It can be done where one is not just existing day to day, but thriving throughout the lifetime.
12. Being ready for learning and ready for life is possible. It is time to move onward and upward. A very hopeful prospect for our children, our schools, and our communities.

References and Suggested Readings

Allen, 1991; Friedman, 2000; Kogan 1999; (Katcher and Williams (1994) (In Geist, 2011).

Allen, J.S., & Klein, R.R. (1996). Ready, set, R.E.L.A.X.: Research based program of relaxation, learning, and self-esteem for children. Watertown, WI: Inner Coaching.

American Academy of Pediatrics (2015). Retrieved on 7/7/15 from http://www.healthychildren.org/English/family-life/family-dynamics/communication-discipline/pages/Normal-Child-Behavior.aspx.

ADTA. American Dance Therapy Association. *Brief Summary of Research on the Effectiveness of Dance/Movement Therapy*. Retrieved on 7/22/15 from http://www.adta.org/Resources/Documents/DMT%20Effectiveness%20research%20handout%202014%20(1).pdf.

APA (Released February 4, 2015). Stress in America: Paying with our health. Retreived 10/2/2016 from http://www.apa.org/news/press/releases/2014/stress-report.pdf.

Badie, R. (July 11, 1993). Dolphin becomes school board target. *The Orlando Sentinel*. Retrieved on 11/25/15 from http://articles.orlandosentinel.com/1993-07-11/news/9307100579_1_aquatron-duso-eastern-religion.

Bartsch, L. (poster presentation). Department of Social Work, Minnesota State University "The Impact of Mindfulness and Relaxation Techniques Implemented Within the Minnesota School Settings: A Program Proposal for Waseca Junior and Senior High School." Retrieved online on 9/4/14 from http://sbs.mnsu.edu/socialwork/graduate/capstone/capstonedoc/bartsch.pdf.

Benson, H., & Klipper, M. (2000). *The Relaxation Response*. New York, NY: Harper Collins.

Benson, H. *Dr. Herbert Benson Quotes*. Retrieved on 7/26/15 from https://www.entheos.com/quotes/by_teacher/Dr.%20Herbert%20Benson.

Black, D.S., & Fernado, R. (2013). Mindfulness training and classroom behavior among lower-income and ethnic minority elementary school children. *Journal of Child and Family Studies*. 22 (1–5), http://link.springer.com/article/10.1007/s10826-013-9784-4.

References and Suggested Readings

Boeree, C.G. (2006). Carl Jung: Personality Theories. Retrieved on 6/13/15 from http://webspace.ship.edu/cgboer/jung.html.

Bransford, J.D. [et al.,] editors. (2004). *How People Learn: Brain, Mind, Experience, and School.* Committee on Developments in the Science of Learning and Committee on Learning Research and Educational Practice, Commission on Behavioral and Social Sciences and Education, National Research Council. Washington, DC: National Academy Press.

Brazelton, T.B. (1992). *Touchpoints.* Reading, MA: Perseus Books

Brazelton, T.B., & Greenspan, S.I. (2000). *The Irreducible Needs of Children: What Every Child Must Have to Grow, Learn, and Flourish.* Cambridge, MA: Perseus Books.

Buckminster Fuller, R., (Quote at beginning of Chapter. 4) Cannon, W. (1939). *The Wisdom of the Body.* New York, NY: W.W. Norton.

Campbell, E. (October 10, 2013). "Research Round-up: Mindfulness in schools Greater." Retrieved on 10/6/2016 from http://greatergood.berkeley.edu/article/item/research_round_up_school_based_mindfulness_programsGood.

Cannon, W. (1939). *The Wisdom of the Body.* New York, NY: W.W. Norton.

Card, N.A. (2012). *Applied Meta Analysis for the Social Science Research.* New York, NY: Guilford Press.

Carpenter. (2001). APA. (February 4, 2015). *Stress in America: Paying with our health.* Retrieved 10/2/16 from http://www.apa.org/news/press/releases/2014/stress-report pdf.

Center for Disease Control. (July 1, 2013). Sleep and sleep disorders; How much sleep do I need? Retrieved on 6/25/15 from http://www.cdc.gov/sleep/about_sleep/how_much_sleep.htm.

Center for Disease Control (CDC). (2014). Retrieved on 11/1/15 from http://www.cdc.gov/violenceprevention/acestudy/.

Chandler, C. (2001). Animal-Assisted Therapy in Counseling and School Settings. ERIC/CASS Digest. ERIC Identifier: ED459404 Publication Date: October, 10 Author: Chandler, Cynthia Source: ERIC Clearinghouse on Counseling and Student Services Greensboro NC.

Chopra, D., & Tanzi R. (2012). *Super Brain: Unleashing the Explosive Power of the Mind to Maximize Health, Happiness, and Spiritual Well-being.* New York, NY: Harmony Books.

Chopra, D., & Tanzi, R. (2015). *Super Genes.* New York: NY, Harmony.

Common Health. see Wilcher below ... Wilcher (1989).

Corbin (2015). Chapter 3 ending.

Counselman, E.F. (2005). Spirit and psyche. *International Journal of Group Psychotherapy.* 55(2), 323–326. Retrieved from http://ezproxy.snhu.edu/login?url=http://search.proquest.com/docview/194779959?accountid=3783.

Counselman, E.F. (April, 2005). Spirit and Psyche. *International Journal of Group Psychotherapy.* 55 (2), 323–326.

Cruz, R.F., & Koch, S. (Spring, 2015). Dance Movement Therapy Program. Received: 8 October, 2014, Accepted: 15 December, 2014. *International Body Psychotherapy Journal The Art and Science of Somatic Praxis.* 14 (1), 10–19

Dacey, DeSalvatore & Robinson (Fall, 1996). The results of teaching middle school students two relaxation techniques as part of a conflict resolution prevention program. *Research in Middle Level Education Quarterly,* 92–102.

Dallas, M.E. (2015). http://www.nlm.nih.gov/medlineplus/news/fullstory_152211.html.
Davidson, R.J., Kabat-Zinn, J., Schumacher, J., Rosenkranz, M., Muller, D., Santorelli, S.F., et al. (2003). Alterations in brain and immune function produced by mindfulness meditation. *Psychosomatic Medicine.* 65, 564–70. DOI: 10.1097/01.PSY.0000077505.67574.E3 [PubMed] [Cross Ref].
Deckro, G.R., Ballinger, K.M., Hoyt, M., Wilcher, M., & et al. (2002). The evaluation of a mind/body intervention to reduce psychological distress and perceived stress in college students. *Journal of American College Health.* 50 (6), 281–287. Retrieved from http://ezproxy.snhu.edu/login?url=http://search.proquest.com/docview/213063327?accountid=3783.
Eckman, P. (2008). *Emotional Awareness.* New York, NY: Holt.
Elkind, D. (2001). *The Hurried Child* (3rd edition). Cambridge, MA: DecapPress.
Fine, A.H. (2010). *Handbook on Animal Assisted Therapy: Theoretical Foundations and Guidelines for Practice.* San Diego, CA: Elsevier.
Foret, M.M., Scult, A., Wilcher, M., Chudnofsky, R., Malloy, L., Hashmemineiad, N., & Park, E.R. (2012). Integrating a relaxation response-based curriculum into a public high school in Massachusetts. *Journal of Adolescence.* 35 (2), 325–332. Doi:10.1016/j.adolescence.2011.08.008
Friesen, L. (2010). Exploring animal-assisted programs with children in school and therapeutic contexts. *Early Childhood Education Journal.* 37 (4), 261–267.
Friedman, E., Thomas, S., & Eddy, T. (2000). Companion animals and human health; physical and cardiovascular influences. In A.L. Podberscek, E.S. Paul, & J.A. Serpell (Eds.), *Companion Animals and Us: Exploring the Relationships Between People & Pets,* 125–142. New York, NY: Cambridge University Press.
Friesen, L., & Delisle, E. (2012). Animal-assisted literacy: A supportive environment for constrained and unconstrained learning. *Childhood Education.* 88 (2), 102–107. Retrieved from http://ezproxy.snhu.edu/login?url=http://search.proquest.com/docview/1492879889?accountid=3783.
Gaab, N., Tallal, P., Kim, H., Lakshmi Narayanan, K., Archie, J.J., Glover, G.H., et al. (2005). Neural correlates of rapid spectrotemporal processing in musicians and nonmusicians. *Annals of the New York Academy of Sciences,* 1060, 82–88.
Gillen, J., & Gillen, L.. (2012) *Yoga Calm for Children: Educating, Heart, Mind, and Body,* Portland Oregon, LLC: Three Peebles Press.
Goleman, D. In Eckman, P. (2008). *Emotional Awareness.* New York, NY: Holt. (quote from page ix).
Gray, P. (2013). *Free to Learn.* New York, NY: Basic Books.
Graydon, A. Retrieved on 11/25/15 from http://www.quoteland.com/author/Aja-Graydon-Quotes/1794/.
Greene, R.W. (Presentation at School Mentaal Health January, 2010). Transforming School Discipline: Bringing Challenging Students Back from the Brink.
Gunzelmann, B. (2004). Hidden dangers within our schools: What are these problems and how can we fix them? *Educational Horizons.* 83 (1), 66–76.
Gunzelmann, B. (2005). Toxic testing: It's time to reflect upon our current testing practices. *Educational Horizons.* 83 (3), 212–200.

Gunzelmann, B. (2008). Hidden problems in failing schools. *Educational Horizons*. 86 (2), 85–97.

Gunzelmann, B. (Fall, 2009). New Era/New Possibilities: Research-Based Education for Equality & Excellence. *Educational Horizons*. 88 (1), 21–27.

Gunzelmann, B. (2010). *Hidden Dangers to Kids Learning: Parent Guide to Cope with Educational Roadblocks.* Lanham, MD: Rowman & Littlefield Education.

Gunzelmann, B. (2008, 2011). *Hidden Dangers: Subtle Signs of Failing Schools* (2nd edition). Lanham, MD: Rowman & Littlefield.

Gunzelmann, B. (2010, 2011). *Hidden Dangers to Kids Learning: Parent Guide to Cope with Educational Roadblocks* (2nd edition). Lanham, MD: Rowman & Littlefield Education.

Gunzelmann, B. (2012). *Barriers to Excellence: Changes Needed for Our Schools.* Lanham, MD: Rowman & Littlefield Education.

Gunzelmann, B. (2013). *Global Voices and Global Visions: Education for Excellence, Understanding, Sustainability.* Lanham, MD: Rowman & Littlefield Education.

Gunzelmann, B. (2015). *School Safety: Developing Safe Schools and Communities for Our Children.* Lanham, MD: Rowman & Littlefield Education.

Gunzelmann, B., & Connell, D. (2006). The new gender gap: Social, psychological, and neuro-biological, and educational perspectives. *Educational Horizons*. 84 (2), 94–101. (Reprint of this article slated to be in Attachment Parenting in 2013.)

Hallowell, E.M. (2011). *Shine: Using Brain Science to Get the Best from Your People.* Boston, MA: Harvard Business Review Press.

Hawkins, D.R. Retrieved on 11/19/15 from http://izquotes.com/quote/343962.

Hagenauer, M.H., Perryman, J.I., Lee, T.M., & Carskadon, M.A. (2009). Adolescent changes in the homeostatic and circadian regulation of sleep. *Developmental Neuroscience*. 31, 276–284.

Hardiman, M. (2001). Connecting brain research with dimensions of learning. *Educational Leadership*. 59 (3), 52–56.

Hoge, E. 9/16/14. Can Meditation Improve Resilience? Evidence from Cells, Cytokines, and Scans.

Hyde, A.L., Maher, J.P., & Elavsky, S. (2013). Enhancing our understanding of physical activity and wellbeing with a lifespan perspective. *International Journal of Wellbeing*, 3 (1), 98–115. doi:10.5502/ijw.v3i1.6

Jung, C. Retrieved on 6/13/15 from http://www.brainyquote.com/quotes/authors/c/carl_jung.html#HMjyluAjqjKVCVDJ.99.

Jung, C. Read more at http://www.brainyquote.com/quotes/authors/c/carl_jung.html#vCGzCDSRqe4b7ymg.99.

Kabat-Zinn, M., & Kabat-Zinn, J. (1977). *Everyday Blessings: The Inner Work of Mindful Parenting.* Zinn. New York, NY: Hyperion.

Kabat-Zinn, J. (2003). Mindfulness-based interventions in context: Past, present ,and future. *Clinical Psychology: Science and Practice*. 144–156.

Kabat-Zinn, J.I., In Hornich-Lisciandro, T. (October, 2013). Mindfullness in education. *The Education Digest*. 79 (2), 66–60.

Khalsa S.B.S., & Gould, J. (2012). *Your Brain on Yoga*. Harvard University Electronic book: New York, NY: Rosetaa Books.

Klatt, M., et al. (2013). Feasibility and preliminary outcomes for Move-into-learning: An arts–based mindfulness classroom intervention. *Journal of Positive Psychology*. 8 (3), 233–241.

Klein, R.J. *School-Based Intervention Using Muscle Relaxation Techniques*. Retrieved 10/27/16 from wwwselectivemutism.org/resources/library/school%20Issues/school%20Based%20Int. (Reprinted on the SMG website with permission of Dr. Klein who is the Author of Ready, set, RELAX.)

Koch, S., Kunz, T., Lykou, S., & Cruz, R. (2014). Effects of dance movement therapy and dance on health-related psychological outcomes: A meta-analysis. *The Arts in Psychotherapy*. 41 (1), 46–64. doi:10.1016/j.aip.2013.10.004.

Langer, E. (1997). *The Power of Mindful Learning*. Reading, MA: Addison-Wesley Publishers.

Larochette, J.G. In Swartz, K. (January 17, 2014). Low-income schools see big benefits in teaching mindfulness. *Mindshift*. PBS & NPR. Retrieved on 11/25/15 from http://ww2.kqed.org/mindshift/2014/01/17/low-income-schools-see-big-benefits-in-teaching-mindfulness/.

Lawrence-Lightfoot, S. (2009). *The Third Chapter: Passion, Risk, and Adventure in the 25 Years After 50*. New York, NY: Sarah Crichton Books,

Levinson, B.M. (1969). *Pet-Oriented Child Psychotherapy*. Springfield, IL: Charles C. Thomas-Publisher, Ltd.

Lowry, R.A. (2011). A Survey of Youth Yoga Curriculums. Temple University. Dissertation no: 3477775, p. 514.

Lythcott-Hiam, J. (2013). Helping or hovering: The effect of Helicopter parenting on college students' well being. *Journal of Child and Family Studies*, New York, NY: Springer Science + Business Media.

Maslow, A. (1971). *Toward a Psychology of Being*. New York, NY: Van Nostrand.

McClelland, D. Retrieved on 6/13/15 from http://www.accelteam.com/human_relations/hrels_06_mcclelland.html.

McDonald, E.S. (January/February, 2010) A quick look into the middle school brain. Principal: 46–47.

McEwen B.S. (2011). Effects of Stress on the Developing Brain. *Cerebrum: the Dana Forum on Brain Science*. 14.

Mead, M. Retrieved on 11/25/15 from http://www.goodreads.com/quotes/122996-children-must-be-taught-how-to-think-not-what-to.

Merton, T. Retrieved on 6/21/09 from http://thinkexist.com/quotation/we_must_make_the_choices_that_enable_us_to/226175.html.

National Sleep Foundation Sleep and Teens Task Force. (2000). Adolescent Sleep Needs and Patterns: Research Report and Resource Guide. Washington: National Sleep Foundation: 1–26.

NIH: National Institute of Health. National Heart Lung and Blood Institute, (2012). Retrieved on 11/21/15 from http://www.nhlbi.nih.gov/health/health-topics/topics/sdd/why.

Novotney, A. (September 2014). Students under pressure. *Monitor on Psychology*. 45 (8).

Organisation for Economic Co-operation and Development: OECD (2012). Programs for International Student Assessment (PISA). 2012 results in focus. Retrieved 10/02/2016 from http://www.oecd.org/pisa/keyfindings/pisa-2012-results-overview.pdf.

Pavlov, I. Retrieved on 7/29/15 from https://www.psychologytoday.com/blog/fulfillment-any-age/201111/15-great-psychology-quotes-and-what-makes-them-great.

Piaget, J. Retrieved on 7/29/15 from http://www.brainyquote.com/quotes/quotes/j/jeanpiaget403394.html.

Ratey, J.J., & Manning, R. (2014). *Go Wild: Free Your Body and Mind from the Afflictions of Civilization*. New York, NY: Little Brown and Company.

Ratey, J., & Hagerman. (2008, 2013). Spark: Supercharge your mental circuits to Beat Stress, Sharpen Your Thinking, Lift Your Mood, and Boost Your Memory and much More. New York, NY: Little Brown & Company.

Resources | Meditation in Schools. Retrieved on 7/26/15 from http:ww.meditationinschools.org/resources/.

Richard, D. (2005). *Explore: The journal of Science and Healing*. New York, NY: ISSN: 1550-8307.1(5), 380–388. DOI:10.1016/j.explore.2005.06.013.

Schermer, V.L. (2003). *Spirit and Psyche: A New Paradigm for Psychology, psychoanalysis, and Psychotherapy*. London: Jessica Kingsley Publishers.

Schultz, D.P., & Schultz, S.E. (2013). *Theories of Personality*. Belmont, CA: Wadsworth.

Schwartz, K. (January 17, 2014). Low-income schools see big benefits in teaching mindfulness. Retrieved 9/8/14 from https://ww2.kqed.org/mindshift/2014/01/17/low-income-schools-see-big-benefits-in-teaching-mindfulness/

Seligman, M. (1996). *The Optimistic Child*. New York, NY: Perennial.

Seligman, M.E. (2011). *Flourish: A Visionary New Understanding of Happiness and Well-Being*. New York, NY: Simon & Schuster.

Seligman, M.E.P. (1990, 1998). *Learned Optimism: How to Change Your Mind and Your Life*. New York, NY: Pocket Books.

Siegel, D.J. (2007). *The Mindful Brain. Reflections and Attunement in the Cultivation of Well-Being*, the chapter was reprinted with permission in 2008 for conference. New York, NY: W.W. Norton.

Siegel, R.D. (2010). *The Mindfulness Solutions: Everyday Practices for Everyday Purpose*. New York, NY: Guilford Press.

Shaywitz, 2003; Simos et.al (2002). In Sousa, 2010, p. 17 ... see full reference for Sousa, 2010.

Slovacek, Tucker, & Pantoja, (2003).

Sousa, D.A. Ed. (2010). *Mind, Brain, & Education: Neuroscience Implications for the Classroom*. Bloomington, IN: Solution Tree Press

Stamm, (2007). Bright from the start.—The simple science-backed way to nurture your child from birth to Age 3, 1–29.

Swartz, K. (January 17, 2014). Low-income schools see big benefits in teaching mindfulness. *Mindshift*. PBS & NPR. Retrieved on 11/25/15 from http://ww2.kqed.org/mindshift/2014/01/17/low-income-schools-see-big-benefits-in-teaching-mindfulness/.

Thompson, R.A. (2014). Stress and child development. *The Future of Children*. 24 (1) Us DHHS.gov ch 12 re exercise for longer life, etc.

Vokell. (1990). Retrieved on 11/3/14 from http://education.purduecal.edu/Vockell/ EdPsyBook/Edpsy4/edpsy4_genetic.htm.
Watts, R. (Feburary 25, 2015). *View Royal's Shoreline School Puts Fitness First*. Retrieved on 7/8/15 from http://www.getsportiq.com/2015/06/view-royals-shoreline-school-puts-fitness-first/.
Weingus, L. (6/02/15). Airline Now Requires New Piolots and Crew to Practice Yoga. Retrieved 7/22/15 from http://www.huffingtonpost.com/2015/06/02/airline-yoga-cabin-crew_n_7494972.html.
Wilcher, M. (2012). *Grab a Tiger by the Toe: Stress Proof Your Child*. Vero Beach, Florida: Inkslinger Press
Willis, J. (Summer 2009). How students' sleepy brains fail them. *Kappa Delta Phi Record*. 45 (4), 158–162.
Willis, J. (2012). *Bad for the Brain*. Retreieved on 10/6/16 from www.edutopia.org/blog/bad-for-brain-unsustainable-models-judy-willis-md.
Willis, J. (2014). Neuroscience reveals that boredom hurts. *Phi Delta Kappan*. 95 (8), 28–32.
Willis, J. (2014) [In Zimmerman, R. (April 10, 2014). Newton Deploys Relaxation Experts to De_Stress community. Common Health Reform & Reality.] Retrieved on 11/23/15 from http://commonhealth.wbur.org/2014/04/newton-deploys-relaxation-experts-to-help-de-stress-community.
Woolfolk, A. (2013). *Educational Psychology* (12th edition). Boston: Allyn & Bacon.
World Health Organization. (July, 2008). Retrieved on 7/29/15 from http://www.who.int/ceh/capacity/Children_are_not_little_adults.pdf.

Notes

CHAPTER 7

1. For specific information on Rogers, Adler's and Erikson's theories please refer to: Myers, D. (2012) Schultz and Schultz (2013)

CHAPTER 8

1. Although there are many who would not agree, many animal species also appear to possess an inner core. Even the hormones and neurotransmitters, the chemicals we associate with human emotions, apparently are remarkably similar across taxa. (Montgomery, 2015, p. 115) More about this when we discuss animals as a possible intervention approach.

2. We might also want to look at our understanding of later life (aging, dying, and death) to better understand the concept of spirit, all that makes us unique as well as all that make us one with humanity and nature.

3. They might have a disorder if they can't sit still or are disruptive or cannot pay attention or read, and so forth. Yes indeed they might, particularly if it interferes with their learning. But they also may be bored, healthy, and energetic, or even not well prepared on all elements for learning readiness or life challenges. Certainly such concerns should be brought to the attention of the child's pediatrician, so that proper assessment can be obtained. But attention should be paid to all of the child's needs physically, cognitively, emotionally, spiritually, and behaviorally.

4. I have written more extensively on this topic of revengeful teachings as a safety concern within our schools in *Developing Safer Schools and Communities for Our Children: The Interdisciplinary Responsibility of Our Time* (Gunzelmann, 2014, p. 194–195).

> "At the core of who we are is the roots of those that have influenced our lives the most and the impact of what they have exposed us to is always there and when the foundation is laid with love and commitment, our lives at some point will reflect that of which we have been taught"—Aja Graydon.

CHAPTER 9

1. Even when an individual experiences physical challenges, even such as paraplegia, there still can be a congruence within the psychological elements of our thoughts, emotions, sense of self, and even behavior. Certainly, physically challenged individuals may well need modifications to assist with their behavioral outputs, but these people are no less capable or prepared to be ready for learning or ready for life. Indeed, it may be because of such challenges that they are more aware of their direction and purpose in life. The technological advances can indeed play a very beneficial role for these individuals to demonstrate their unique and often superior abilities. Such individuals are great examples of the interface between behavior and the environment.

CHAPTER 10

1. For more specific information on the environmental impacts including the larger community, cultural, political, and economic situations, the reader may want to refer to my previous books listed in the suggested readings and references.
2. For example, gym classes are often cut way down particularly in high school, when students may be required to take gym one or two semesters out of four years! Lunch periods may consist of only 15–20 minutes, including time to wait in line, cleanup after eating, and getting to one's next class. Start times begin earlier due to bus schedules and classroom space as opposed to the need for sleep for the children to learn optimally, and so forth!

About the Author

Betsy Gunzelmann recently retired from her position of professor of psychology at Southern New Hampshire University after twenty years, fifteen years of which she was the chairperson of the Psychology Department.

She has worked as a psychologist, educator, and parent for more than thirty-five years, dealing with issues hindering children's education.

Dr. Gunzelmann plans to continue her research and writing more intensively upon retirement.

www.ingramcontent.com/pod-product-compliance
Lightning Source LLC
Chambersburg PA
CBHW021304240426
43669CB00041B/140